Problems to Go, Problems to Solve

Problems to Go, Problems to Solve

Dominic W. Moreo

Writers Club Press

San Jose New York Lincoln Shanghai

Problems to Go, Problems to Solve

Writers Club Press
an imprint of iUniverse.com, Inc.

For information address:
iUniverse.com, Inc.
620 North 48th Street, Suite 201
Lincoln, NE 68504-3467
www.iuniverse.com

ISBN: 0-595-12731-2

Printed in the United States of America

To the many students of mine who engaged in the ping-pong
of listening, response, and still more volleys
in the never-ending game of learning, my delight
and ever-lasting gratitude.

Where observation is concerned,
chance favors only the *prepared mind*.
                              —Louis Pasteur

The *mind* is never passive; it is a perpetual
activity, delicate,s receptive, responsive to
stimulus. You cannot postpone its life until
you have sharpened it. Whatever interest
attaches to your subject-matter must be
evoked here and now; whatever powers you are
strengthening in the pupil, must be exercised
here and now; whatever possibilities of
mental life your teaching should impart,
must be exhibited here and now. That is the
golden rule of education, a very difficult rule to follow.
                              —Alfred North Whitehead
                              The Aims of Education

Contents

Preface .... *x*

Part One Mental Software xvi

   1 Tools of the Trade *1*

   2 Ladders and Metaphors *15*

Part Two Mental Applications And Exercises 40

   3 Into the Problem Pits! *41*

   4 What If...? *49*

Part Three Mental Wallpapers 53

   5 What is the Problem? *54*

   6 Which One to Buy, When, Where? *63*

   7 Why Tax Me? *71*

   8 The Hiding Hand *84*

   9 Hatfields and McCoys! *94*

   Bibliography *98*

   About the Author *128*

Preface

Problems, problems everywhere. Problems to go, problems to tackle. Problems unlimited in number and scope. Problems in two basic varieties, those that come and go of their own accord, and those that persist and demand solutions. Some may deny that particular problems exist, still others while acknowledging that problems exist, suggest a detour since the issues are insoluble. And finally despite our thoughts, efforts and excuses, there are problems that slide into conflicts.

Where does the supply of "problems" come from? Throughout time, the main sources have been errors and mistakes from the daily commonplaces of life. More importantly, given the daily volume of mistakes, how have individuals, groups, corporations, institutions, governments and societies advanced? Perhaps one answer is that no sooner have mistakes made their appearance than problem solving skills blossom. Problems, accidents and mistakes are challenges by any other name. Thus whether mistakes occur by inadvertence or by design, fertile minds respond with solutions.

Today thanks to the global village of worldwide communications of satellites and the Internet, new problems shout for attention. In the past, screaming headlines announced earthquakes that struck San Francisco, Mexico, China and Soviet Armenia; hurricanes lashed South Carolina and South Florida; winter blizzards dumped snow, in turn followed by spring floods; while mountain tops such as Mt. St. Helens and Mt. Pinatubo blew their stacks.

Down to earth, the nightly newscasts tell of more typical problems and conflicts that daily assault our urban senses: crack, AIDS and AZT, child abuse, abortion, the homeless, crack babies, violent labor strikes, riots, murders, inflation, recession, corporate lay-offs, pesticides on apples, drive by shootings, and church arson fires. By the late 1990s, some of the above have diminished.

Across the land our arteries of movement are clogged with traffic. Along with auto emissions the air is laced with smog, and acid rain, while the rivers, beaches and harbors are befouled with agricultural run-offs, pesticides, sludge and medical wastes. Meanwhile both garbage and toxic wastes pile up. Recycling arrives, apparently, none too soon.

On the economic front, within the marketplace of daily solutions, *bankruptcy* is a special device in correcting past mistakes of shoddy and overpriced products. A business firm unable or unwilling to meet consumer preferences faces bankruptcy when creditors demand payment for products and services rendered. Bankruptcy clears the economy by releasing labor, property, facilities, and materials to new uses. While particular business firms and workers incur the costs of correcting mistakes, consumers and society benefit by the creation of new ventures, new products and new jobs.

On the political front, politicians play their games of collecting campaign funds, while banking and financial scandals, Whitewater investigations, White House sexual misbehaviors, the usual pork-barrel politics, and other diversions of tax funds that lead to the unhappy conclusion that the federal government may create more problems than it solves.

On the disaster front, terrorists, overseas and domestically, ply their trade as the bombings of Pan Am 747 over Lockerbie, Scotland, the World Trade Center in New York City and the Oklahoma federal building attest. Again, starvation sweeps across Ethiopia, Somalia and Rwanda as the country of the week on our nightly television news draws on our compassion and donations.

Meanwhile in the spring of 1989, flickers of freedom were extinguished in Beijing, China as student calls for democracy were silenced and crushed by tanks.

In the fall of 1989, the story of the century occurred. For forty years, the Iron Curtain had been rusting. Then as the fleeing East Germans fled through Hungary into West Germany, the rusted curtain disintegrated. As the exodus of people voting with their feet turned to floodtide, the Berlin Wall crashed.

As walls and curtains came tumbling down, leaders fell and like Humpty Dumpty, they could not be made whole. Like the emperor without clothes, the communist leaders suddenly had no legitimacy to rule. Even a protester in Moscow caught the winds of change with a placard that read: "Seventy Years on the Road to Nowhere." Seventy years of unlimited mistakes and errors. The dogmas of Marxism and Leninism that justified central control of daily life appeared in full retreat. A monumental error of national and international scope had finally been placed on worldview. Who would be next?

Yet, no sooner does one issue vanish from public consciousness than several new ones clamor for attention. Conflict in the Persian Gulf, for example, brought war, environmental spills and terrorism. Somalia and Haiti became trouble spots. Then Yugoslavia disintegrated into bloodshed and "ethnic cleansing" before our eyes. Curiously, the grim historical leitmotif of the twentieth century may be, *From Sarajevo to Sarajevo, 1914 & 1991*. Finally the United States joined other N.A.T.O. countries in sending troops to Bosnia to enforce the December 1995 Dayton peace accords. Then another part of Yugoslavia, Kosovo, erupted into civil war with more ethnic cleansing.

On the domestic front, crimes such as murder, rape, child molestation, drunk driving and street mugging are serious threats to the social fabric. Similarly drive-by-shootings are a menace to daily life. But how do we solve these social problems in whole or in part? At what level? At what benefit? At what cost in terms of freedoms lost, lives lost and dollars wasted?

Discourtesy and incivility are the errors and breakdowns of social life. On the roads, for example, on streets and freeways car drivers cross lanes without signaling, cut in front of others to exit, tailgate, pass on the right, run red lights and at times shoot other motorists. For many cowboys and cowgirls of the highways, common courtesy is seen as something from the age of Jurassic Park. How do we solve these social problems?

To the human eye, the supply of natural and human disasters seems infinite. Despite the foregoing, problems are the lifeblood of any dynamic society. A society without problems is a nation of the dead.

As noted, many problems flow from mistakes, errors, and accidents that daily afflict our personal lives. By the million, we daily choose to buy, sell, move, trade, change jobs, marry, invest, travel and make many more decisions. Out of these daily choices, success and misfortune flow. Mistakes abound. Some can be undone, others modified while still others are irreversible like spilt drinks.

In the classroom, errors multiply daily as students grapple with math problems, the correct pronunciation of words, and the proper way to develop an expository paragraph, or the delivery of a persuasive speech. How do students master clear thinking, clear writing, and clear speaking free of errors and mistakes? At once, or by due practice?

But graduation from high school and college does not provide a vaccination against human errors. All too often mistakes and errors follow us into adulthood as check accounts fail to balance, income tax forms confuse, phone numbers are misdialed, and VCR programming mystifies.

But for Americans when confronted by personal, group and societal problems the usual response is to roll up one's sleeves and pitch-in. Problems may come and go and sometimes take on the appearance of a "bad news/good news" by-play, yet the need to understand, to cope, and to solve problems is as acute and as necessary as breathing.

As to form, problems more often than not are messy rather than neat and tidy. Thus problems at times may appear as chaos. But regardless of form, they present a challenge to individuals, to groups and to institutions to tackle and solve them. Once "solved," new problems are born. And the social cycle of mistakes and problems begins anew. The principle of the "hiding hand" in chapter eight speaks to this human resourcefulness in problem solving.

Aside from number and form, another aspect of societal problems is their size and scale. Given the enormity of some problems the temptation is to turn to governments for solutions. But large problems may well be sub-divided and thus made manageable by individuals, groups and the marketplace without government intervention.

To stand under an avalanche is not the best way to ski. To drown in a sea of problems is no way to swim. Who would prefer a car in motion without a steering wheel, a ship plowing the seas with a disabled rudder, a DC-10 in flight over Iowa with a disabled tail section? Hence the need for a shopping kit of mental tools. Why?

Raw materials like current problems remain in that raw state unless with the aid of mental concepts, models, rubrics and scaffolding, these inert "ores" are turned into intermediate and final "products." In similar fashion, "rough" facts, information and statistics are turned into knowledge. The pay-offs of this mental endeavor are the smiles of illumination, that is, of understanding how and why people behave and how and why economies and societies function well or ill. Understanding yields a measure of control of our destiny. Otherwise, as Ralph Waldo Emerson noted, events are in the saddle.

Historically in the 18th and 19th centuries came the new inventions, new discoveries that solved a host of problems from John Harrison's solution of the longitude issue, James Watt's improved steam engine, the coming of the railroads, the telegraph, electric light and Louis

Pasteur's discoveries in applied bacteriology and the process of *pasteurization*. In the 20th century, a series of medical breakthroughs from antibiotics to organ transplants, the construction of mammoth projects such as the Panama Canal, Hoover Dam, the Brooklyn Bridge, unlocking the atom, going to the moon, the computer, and exploring the depths of the oceans are a few of the major problems tackled and solved by individuals, groups, corporations and government.

Then how does one prepare the mind? By trial and error experiences? By parental guidance? By the example of mentors? By study? Is there a vaccine that prevents mistakes and errors? Can one earn major league sports' salaries of millions without having played a single game? Can one make a career of finding quick fixes and short cuts? For most people there remain only the slow, methodical and sometimes painful steps of practice and guidance. In short, errors can be minimized and the mind honed by study.

What follows then is a primer on finding our way through the labyrinth of problems from the personal to the public. *Part One* provides an introduction to mental software akin to Whitehead's general ideas while *Part Two* invites the reader to apply the software to problem solving. *Part Three* provides a series of mental wallpapers as necessary background. Further, the bibliography is an invitation for study, reflection and hands-on problem solving. All in all, the three parts and bibliography serve as the metaphorical Ariadne's thread in finding our way through the maze of today's social, economic and political life. In the process the mind is sharpened and prepared for further problem solving.

Part One

Mental Software

1 Tools of the Trade

Before a home, apartment complex, plant or skyscraper can be built, a number of things must be done. At the outset, competent engineers, architects, and contractors must initiate planning. Next the recruitment of skilled labor. Thirdly the flows of materials to the site must be scheduled. Lastly for large and tall structures, the need for tools, cranes, elevators and scaffolding is essential.

Pursuing this last point, the mind requires mental scaffolding not unlike the construction of anything of value. What follows is an array of mental tools such as ladders, metaphors, brackets, and spectrums that serve the mind as so much scaffolding. Along with information, and evidence, the tools permit the handling of the buzz of information much as kitchen gloves and pot handles permit us to pick up "hot" items.

This chapter introduces and defines the concepts; the following chapter presents hands-on exercises of most of these same tools of the trade. Then chapter three invites the reader to pursue several issues in problem solving. In turn, chapter four puts a new spin on old problems by raising "what if" scenarios.

At the outset we mention the prime gift of society and civilization: the ability to speak, think and write in a *common language* and thus end our isolation from our fellow human beings. Helen Keller's life illustrated the triple prison of not speaking, not hearing, and not seeing. Only by extraordinary effort, and courage did she reach out for communion with others. We take language so much for granted until we arrive in a foreign country unable to speak and are thus reduced to smiles, gestures and signs.

To begin with we have:

>>1.   the concept and the metaphor of *the house of language*: as opposed to the typical tripartite usages of language by slang, informal and formal. The house metaphor offers a functional perspective. The house has four levels:

* **Attic**: here the *symbols and slogans* of the culture enjoy an airy loft echoing their high level abstraction.

* **Upper floor**: here the *higher thoughts* of religion, philosophy, poetry, proverbs and maxims enjoy residence.

* **Street floor**: the *mundane transactions* of the marketplace and government swirl; social gossip; jargon—the special sub-languages of government bureaucrats, educators, the military, scientists, as well as sports figures and Hollywood denizens.

* **Basement**: here *unpopular ideas* take root; profanity enjoys its base; slang and argot thrive away from respectability until such time as they move into the mainstream of public speech; *unpopular and popular behaviors* of criminals, spies, terrorists reduced to word coinage of symbols: Al Capone, James Bond and Carlos the Jackal.

>>2.   concept: an abstraction ladder in which a set of particulars, terms, and nouns are arranged from the most specific to the most general. A triangle superimposed over the ladder would illustrate the concept more clearly. Two forms of thinking by individuals that implicitly use the ladder are deductive and inductive reasoning. In the former case, an individual begins with a hypothesis or theory, or a general statement, and then proceeds to search for evidence either to challenge or to fit the hypothesis. On the other hand,

inductive reasoning takes place when a set of particular events, phenomena, and numbers lead an individual to infer a general statement of explanation or hypothesis.

Caution: the danger is to avoid either the airy heights of high level abstraction devoid of contact with particulars, or on the other hand to collect endless particulars to no purpose. Effective reasoning and problem solving involves moving up and down the abstraction ladder.

>>3.   game theory that postulates a closed-ended situation involving two or more participants with three likely outcomes:
* **Positive-sum game**: in which all participants gain to one degree or another; the supreme example: industrial growth and modernization since the 18th Century in Western Europe and the United States lifting standards of living.
* **Zero-sum game**: in which one set of participants gains at the expense of others; examples: normal traffic lights; gambling in which the winning of some, are the losses of others; theft, burglary, robbery, extortion, and bribery in which the criminals' gains are at the expense of others.
* **Negative-sum game**: in which almost all participants lose in varying degrees; examples: a drug infested street or neighborhood; four-way stop signs; widespread pollution of air and oceans; a global nuclear war.

>>4.   concept: *bracketing* in which a goal is approached too strenuously or too lackadaisically; subsequent effort leads closer and closer to the goal. The term comes from artillery and mortar firing in which a target receives an overshot and undershot, subsequent calibration locates the target. The following shot strikes the target.

Other examples involve collective bargaining in which labor and management present polar offers setting the boundaries for negotiations.

Also it appears in another setting in which theory permits us to see ahead of the target while trial and error inches us forward. Still another illustration involves, for example, which economic system hits the target of consumer demand more often, a price driven marketplace or a centrally planned one? See chapters six and seven on this issue of minimizing mistakes in number and scale as one way to succeed.

>>5.   concept: convergent/divergent forces in which centripetal forces vie against centrifugal forces within society. Example: civil war (divergence out of control) rends the society. Normally in any society, both forces are held in a fluid balance. Our national motto recognizes and illustrates this truth: E Pluribus Unum (diversity within unity).

For example, in terms of economic production: *productive* efforts lead to positive sum situations, more for all: a stabilizing and convergent force; while predatory efforts lead to zero-sum outcomes: gambling, criminal activities, and civil suits for alleged injuries: these are destabilizing and divergent forces.

Finally, in terms of mental processes, convergent thinking is linear thought, continuous, one thing at a time. While divergent thinking is roundabout, zigzagging, intuitive, discontinuous.

>>6.   concept: whole/part relationships: there are two aspects to this dimension, one static and the other dynamic. As to the first we postulate the following questions: 1) Is the whole greater than the sum of the parts? 2) Is the whole simply the sum of the parts? 3) Is the whole less than the sum of the parts? Dynamically, do a series of small events accumulate to render a change in degree or kind? If the latter, is the whole transformed by its parts?

Examples: is society the sum of the dead, the living and posterity? Metaphorically, is society a collection of still photographs or an ongoing but never-ending movie? Further is the sum of individual self-interests equal to the public interest? Also, is an individual life merely the sum of bodily organs? What is death, then?

Dynamically, a domino effect postulates that a small act or two leads to a long chain of events with profound or substantial effects. Examples: in a fog and ice bound freeway, one skidding car leads to multiple car collisions; the following proverb illustrates the notion:

For want of a nail, the shoe was lost;
For want of a shoe, the horse was lost;
For want of a horse, the rider was lost;
For want of a rider, the battle was lost;
For want of a battle, the kingdom was lost!

Which of the above three whole/part relationships applies to the fog example, and the want of a nail?

>>7.   concept: effect—in which overlapping ideas, products, practices, and systems temporarily or permanently co-exist. Some examples:

*	Salk polio vaccine	Sabin polio vaccine
*	sailing ships	steam propelled ships
*	propeller airplanes	jet airplanes
*	US	USSR (before 1991)

>>8.   concept of *value-added spectrum: From Information to Meaning*

What					
Who	today's/yesterday's/ analysis/opinion = **meaning/**				
When	news news				**action**
???					

_____ >>>>>

???					>>>>
Where					
How many	"spot" + update + context + conclusions= **meaning**				
How much	news			or [jumping to	
Why				conclusions]	
	1	2	3	4	5

The above spectrum is an example of the economist's value-added spectrum that is applicable to all economic and social activity. Consider as an example, the process from raw to finished product with its application to the planting of wheat, its harvesting, transportation, milling, further transportation, baking into bread and final deliverance to the supermarket. In short, the sum of each stage's value-added equals the final price of the good. Above we apply the concept to the media to reveal how primitive the press and television news industry are. By and large they offer us a very limited step one and a faulty step four.

>>9.   concept: relevant range spectrum of problem solving: to save time and to direct our efforts to what is feasible, one must determine quickly not the abstract ends of the spectrum, from A to Z, but the actual more limited range of opportunities, or possibilities. The speedometer in a typical automobile helps us to illustrate the concept. While it states an abstract 0 to 120 mph, for city driving the relevant range would be 20 to 40 mph, for freeway driving, 55 to 75 mph.

There are occasional pure examples of living and operating at the fringes. Automobiles in museums operate at the zero end. In terms of problem solving, the Soviet Union until very recently did not permit private businesses in any forms, (except as black markets) hence the central government handed down all the solutions to major and minor problems in that society. Our society on the other hand is a blend of marketplace and government problem solving.

[A_____/issues/_____Z]
/Relevant Range/

>>10. concept: a metaphor for problem solving—*playing the game of baseball*—in running to first base, one gathers information, statistics, and other pertinent evidence. Proceeding to second base, the evaluation stage subjects the evidence to the test of a hypothesis, principles or values. Moving to third base, conclusions and choices are made. To run home and score is to take action or implement the analysis.

Caution: jumping to conclusions by running to third base is a human propensity, to voice an opinion *without* the facts, *without* a review, and *without* analysis. But you then have *no runs, no hits, but lots of errors!*

>>11. concept: *a precis of problem solving*:

A. What is the problem?

1. what are its *boundaries*? personal, family, or societal level?
2. *how many people* are affected?
3. what is the *nature* of the problem?
   a). economic
   b). political
   c). social
   d). medical

            e). psychological

            f). military

            g). scientific

         4. what is its *scope*?

            a). local

            b). regional

            c). national

            d). international

B. Is *information* available?

     1. *how reliable* is it?

     2. is it *primary or secondary* data?

     3. form: expert testimony; studies; statistics; biographies; polls; press interviews; legislative hearings; election results, etc.?

     4. sources: libraries, universities, think tanks, and laboratories?

     5. specific sources: yellow pages, atlases, dictionaries, almanacs, abstracts, encyclopedia, computer data bases?

C. What principles, values, or goals are in contention? What are the distractions?

     1. whose property or income?

     2. whose freedom?

     3. whose job?

     4. whose privacy?

     5. are values in collision?

     6. are values complementary?

     7. are there detours? blind alleys?

     8. are there hidden premises?

     9. are there hidden agendas?

     10. are there "no contests"?

     11. what tricks of propaganda are diverting the search for solutions?

     12. what errors of reasoning are side-tracking the search?

D. What are the options?

    1. *source*:
       a). by private or public agencies
       b). by individual or voluntary groups
    2. *duration*:
       a). an immediate band-aid
       b). a long run solution
    3. *form*:
       a). temporary/ad hoc
       b). permanent/general

E. Actions:
    1. the consequences of action/non-action?
    2. the problem solved? postponed?
    3. or back to "square one"?

>>12. concept: *first questions*—they are those critical questions that guide and focus our searches for answers much as a flashlight in a dark room illuminates our way by shedding light on some items while others remain in the dark; there are two types of questions: a) *"nuts and bolts"* that are usually devoid of emotions; and b) *"coloring"* questions that tint (like sunglasses) our selection and evaluation of facts and opinions; the questions that follow amplify those presented above in the previous section.

A. "Nuts and Bolts" Questions:
    1. are the *assumptions* or premises of the problem or argument stated or hidden?
    2. is the *analogy* appropriate?
    3. are the facts *exceptions to the rule*?
    4. is the statistical polling sample a *random one*?
    5. what is the *size* of the polling sample?
    6. can an *alternate explanation* fit the facts?

7. does the solution(s) confuse what *ought-to-be* with what is *feasible*?
8. is the "first best" solution feasible?
9. what are the *trade-offs*? [more/less]
10. will the solution(s) have *side-effects*?

B. "Coloring" Questions:

1. does *nature or nurture* shape human behavior primarily? equally?
2. what does the individual owe if anything to society? to the family?
3. what did Horace Mann have in mind when he stated: "Be ashamed to die until you have won some victory for humanity."
4. is freedom:
   a) doing what you like?
   b) doing what comes easiest?
   c) doing what you must do?
   d) doing what you ought to do?
5. what is the best way to secure freedom, prosperity and order in society? for individuals? for families? for society?
   i. by urging altruistic behavior?
   ii. by urging self-interest?
   iii. by urging anarchy?
   iv. by urging group goals?
6. what is the relationship between private and public matters?
7. what is the relationship between the governed and the governors? (part and whole?)
8. what is the relationship of the law to morals and customs?
9. is the pursuit of happiness the highest goal?
10. what is the shape or form of a good society?

comment: the list is not meant to be exhaustive but suggestive of the questions that when properly raised save time, by directing one's efforts in the search and evaluation stages. Of course, the notion that "we need more information" while legitimate may also be used as a delaying tactic. Since *perfect information* in a finite time will never be available, at some point, the analysis must be completed with whatever data are at hand.

>>13. concept: *first principle*: a guide, doctrine, law, truth, or motivating force upon which other actions are based; a rule of conduct. Some examples are:
A. Common Sense:
   1. "live and let live"
   2. "every person has a right to his or her say"
   3. "you're no better than I am"
   4. "there ought to be a law to…"
   5. "you just got to educate them to…"
   6. "hey, let's be fair about this…"
   7. "practice what you preach"
   8. "tell the truth"
   9. "honesty is the best policy"
B. Proverbs and Maxims:
   1 "when the cat is away, the mice will play"
   2 "an apple a day will keep the doctor away"
   3 "variety is the spice of life"
   4 "things will get worse before they ge better"
   5 "a stitch in time saves nine"
C. Attitudes & Dispositions:
   1. "all politicians are crooked"
   2. "people are basically good"
   3. "people are no damn good, they are always letting you down!"
   4. "never stick your neck out"
   5. "it's only book learning"
   6 "history is bunk"

      7 "there's a sucker born every minute"
      8 "you can't trust those people"
  D. Religious & Moral Principles:
     1. the Golden Rule
     2. faith, hope and charity
     3. the Ten Commandments
     4. the Seven Deadly Sins
     5. truth and honesty
  E. Business Principles:
     1. private property
     2. free enterprise (start a business)
     3. fair competition
     4. anti-trust (monopoly) laws
     5. profit motive
  F. Political Principles:
     1. Declaration of Independence
     2. US Constitution
        a). separation of powers
        b). checks and balances
        c). federalism: 10th Amendment
     3. Bill of Rights
     4. life, liberty & pursuit of happiness
     5. majority rule

    comment: first principles and first questions if they are to be of value must be raised *before* an investigation begins; otherwise if they are raised after decisions are made, if at all, they are *dead*, not first, principles like so much spilt milk; hence most proverbs fall into this category of cliche and language adornment rather than as a guide to action.

>>14. concept: *types of arguments*

 1. *"nuts and bolts"* approach: one that is usually free of emotions, political and religious ballast, hence playing the game of reason is employed.
  a). "Doctor, what do I have?"
  b). "How do I get a job?"
  c). "Who will fix the TV?"
  d). "Which store has the best buys?"
  e). "Let's take a cruise?"
  f). "Which college should we choose?"
  g). "Which agency can help?"

 2. *polemics*: a speech, article or book that vigorously proposes or opposes an idea, program, doctrine or issue, for example, some recent and current public topics:
  a). abortion
  b). capital punishment
  c). affirmative action
  d). nuclear free zone
  e). politically correct views
  f). presidential line item veto
  g). federal housing for the homeless

 3. *pure game of reason*: an exercise in mental gymnastics made all the more profitable *if a substantial fund of knowledge* and tested-experiences are available:
  a). If Hitler had won the Second World War, what would life be like today in the United States?
  b). If Lenin had not launched the second Russian revolution in 1917, what effect would this have had on Hitler's possible invasion of England in 1940? On the United States subsequently?
  c). If Napoleon had not lived, would events have been different in the nineteenth century?

d). If England and France had recognized the South early in the Civil War, what might have occurred?

e). If the populations of India and the United States were swapped permanently on January 1st, what would the form and shape of the economy and political system in each country look like after ten years?

4. *symbolic issues*: there are two varieties here. On the one hand, you appeal to the already converted whether it be over religious or political matters, hence, these appeals are mental and emotional strokings of the true believers, or booster shots of righteousness, etc. The other variety occurs when a particular issue is but a surrogate for other issues:

a). The Populist Revolt of the 1890s and Prohibition were over the more fundamental shift of economic and political influence from Main Street to urban America.

b). School busing, crime in the streets, and drugs were issues from the 1960s onward masking social class cleavages.

c). The defeat of Robert Bork's nomination to the US Supreme Court by the US Senate masked a hidden agenda of opposition to the downsizing of the federal government's role and scope in daily life of the country.

Lastly this catalog of concepts does not exhaust the treasures of the mental tool box. Further treasures and pleasures await the active use of reason by a prepared mind.

2 Ladders and Metaphors

Now we turn to the equivalent of baseball's spring training sessions: a mental warm-up. With the preceding chapter as an introduction, we present a series of mental aerobics and mental images.

What follows are the pictorial illustrations of the concepts enumerated in the preceding chapter. Following each illustration are a set of exercises to drive home each concept and to lay the groundwork for the following chapters.

1. House of Language
2. Abstraction Ladder A
3. Geographical Abstraction Ladder B
4. Game Theory
5. Bracketing Concept
6. Convergent/Divergent Social Forces Concept
7. Whole/Part Relationships
8. Sidling-Effect Concept
9. Value-Added Spectrum
10. Game of Problem Solving

1. Metaphorical House of Language

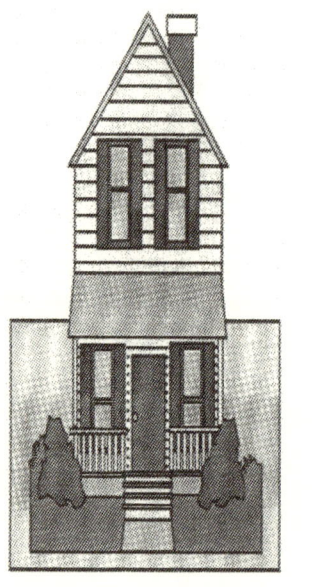

Attic

Upstairs

Street-level

Basement

1 House of Language Exercises

Attic: fill in additional examples

Symbols

1. people: Washington,_____,_____
2. numbers: 1776, _____,_____
3. words: freedom, _____,_____
4. designs: flag, _____,_____
5. places: Mt. Rushmore, _____,_____

6. slogans: Remember Pearl Harbor,_____,_____
7. gestures: V sign in WWII, _____,_____
8. trademarks: GM, AT&T, _____,_____,_____
9. formulas: $a^2+b^2=c^2$, _____,_____

Upstairs: fill in with appropriate questions & examples.

Philosophy & Poetry

1. When birds die where do they go?
2. Why is there pain?
3. Why does evil exist?
4. _____.

Aphorisms

1. "Fools rush in where angels fear to tread."
     Alexander Pope
2. "The road to hell is paved with good intentions."
     William James
3. "To live life to the end is no childish task."
     Boris Pasternak
4. "To be alive at all is to have scars."
     John Steinbeck
5. _____.

Proverbs

1. You can lead a horse to water but can't make him drink
2. Give him an inch, he'll take an arm.
3. Things have got to get worse before they get better.
4. If you have to explain a joke, don't.
5. _____.

Street Level

Transactions of Daily Life

1. "Fill it up with premium."
2. "Give me 2 lbs of steak, 2 gallons of milk, etc."
3. "What time is it, I have an appointment at 3:00PM."
4. "From the catalog, I'd like to order the…"

5. _____.

Euphemism

1. "May I have the white meat (breast) of the chicken."
2. "He bought the farm (died).
3. "The patient in Room 107 expired (died).
4. "Mr. Jones died of natural causes (cancer).
5. _____.

Gossip

1. "Did you hear the latest about Susan…"
2. _____.

Sarcasm

1. "Where did you get those clothes at Goodwill?"
2. "I suppose it runs in the family, like father, like son."
3. "Keep drinking and I'll attend your funeral."
4. _____.

Spoofs

1. **Mad Magazine**
2. _____. 3. _____.

Satire

1. *Saturday Night Live:TV*
2. **Gulliver's Travels; Animal Farm**
3. _____. 4. _____. 5. _____.

Underground

Ideas

1. new ideas in science and politics remain out of sight and percolate until they surface; (spies and terrorists also remain out of sight but not necessarily with new ideas)
2. _____. 3. _____.

Profanity

1. that S.O.B has the nerve to…

2. you can go to &%#!*!

3. _____. 4. _____. 5. _____.

Expletives

1. "Oh, my God......!" (when death strikes)

2. "***++++!" (when a hammer hits your finger!)

3. _____. 4. _____. 5. _____.

2 Abstraction Ladder A

High Level Abstraction	Infinity
	Earth
	USA
Mid-Level Abstraction	Washington
	Seattle
Low-Level Abstraction	Jane Doe

2 Abstraction Ladder A exercises:

In the following sets assign the number 1 to the most specific, or the smallest, or the lowest, and so on to the most general, largest and highest or abstract of terms.

_____"Bessie"
_____Livestock
_____Wealth
_____Farm Asset
_____A cow

_____South America
_____Brazil
_____A coffee plantation
_____Western Hemisphere
_____Juan Valdez (in a coffee ad)
_____A producers' co-operative

_____Wesley Harrison
_____national farm problem
_____Hanes Farm
_____Cotton growing
_____Southern California

_____Mary is a useful person.
_____Yesterday morning, Mary washed the dishes, ironed and watched TV.
_____Mary likes to cook.
_____Mary enjoys listening to her CDs.
_____Mary is a real American.

_____I like driving better than flying.
_____I like old Ford Mustang cars.
_____I like American cars better than foreign ones.
_____I like my green 1967 Mustang convertible.

_____I like to travel.

_____Jim keeps all our mechanical appliances in working order.
_____Jim is a mechanical genius.
_____Jim is very handy with tools.
_____Jim is a 100% real American lad.
_____Jim is an awfully useful person to have around.
_____Yesterday, Jim replaced a spark plug in the lawn mower.
_____Jim keeps the TV in working condition.

3. Geographical Abstract Labber B

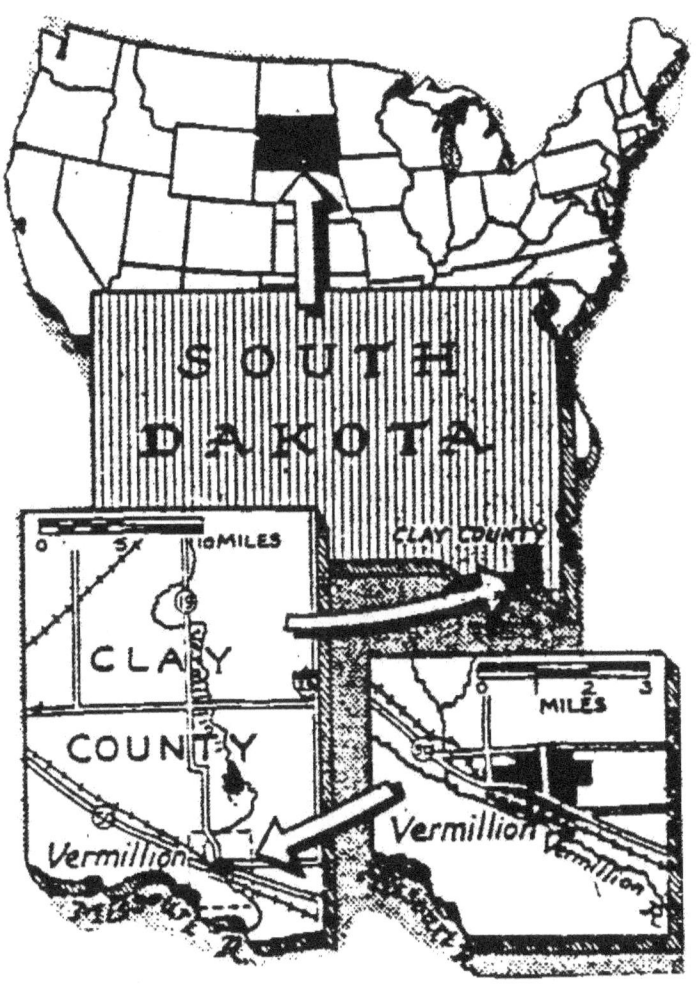

3 Geographical Abstraction Ladder B exercises.

The same instructions as for Ladder A. What library and other sources would provide answers for the following?

A by population	B by area	C by annual homicide rates
_____Chicago	_____Chicago	_____Chicago
_____Detroit	_____Detroit	_____Detroit
_____Los Angeles	_____Los Angeles	_____Los Angeles
_____Miami	_____Miami	_____Miami
_____New York	_____New York	_____New York
_____Washington	_____Washington	_____Washington

D	E
_____Ireland	_____Antarctica
_____Eastern Hemisphere	_____Fluorocarbon Gases
_____Europe	_____Amazon forest fires
_____The Universe	_____Ozone hole
_____Stephen Dedalus	_____Greenhouse Effect
_____County Cork	_____automobile exhausts
_____Dublin	

In the following line sets of 1 & 2, insert the number that is *higher* on the abstraction ladder in the blank space.

_____1. "we ran like the dickens!"   2. strategic withdrawal
_____1. television   2. radio
_____1. knowledge   2. experience
_____1. railroad   2. transportation
_____1. energy business   2. oil company
_____1. principles   2. facts
_____1. New York Times   2. communications

_____1. vehicle specialist   2. car washer
_____1. talking   2. thinking
_____1. sanitary engineer   2. garbage collector
_____1. looking   2. seeing

4. Game Theory

Negative-sum game

[All lose in varying degrees]

Zero-sum game

[Some win, some lose;
more for me, less for you]

Positive-sum game

[All win in varying degrees]

4 Game Theory exercises

Identify which game is applicable to each situation.

(+) *positive-sum;*

(O) *zero-sum*

[also popularly known as the "trade-off"];

(-) *negative-sum.*

_____Los Angeles Dodgers 4, New York Mets 3.

_____For the economy more guns means less butter.

_____A normal traffic light.

_____World wide nuclear war.

_____The condition of US versus Germany in May 1945.

_____A four-way stop sign.

_____While the dollar climbed, the yen fell.

_____Panic by depositors leading to bank closure.

_____First come, first served (others not served).

_____As interest rates fell, bond prices rose.

_____More capital investment now means less consumption.

_____But over time, more capital investment means higher incomes.

_____Two-way stop signs.

_____Rock concerts with arena seating (no reserved seats).

_____As the German mark rose, the dollar fell.

_____Freeway gridlock during evening peak rush hours.

_____Foreign governments defaults of US bank loans

_____Trade of work for goods with money as intermediary.

_____More truthfulness means greater anger.

_____Personal bankruptcy (creditors lose).

_____Home burglary of valuables.

_____Declining work ethic, declining capital investment and runaway inflation.

_____Bitter divorce over custody and property division.

_____The law of diminishing marginal utility.

_____Barter of goods for goods.

_____Public knowledge.

_____More kindness means less honesty.

_____Winner takes all in poker.

_____Money as a medium of exchange, as a measure of value and as a store of value in a stable economy.

_____Given OPEC's oil quotas, an increased quota for Kuwait means a decrease for the other members.

5. Bracketing Concept

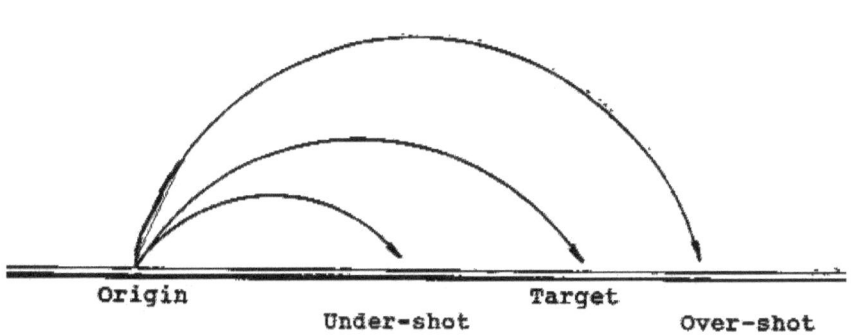

Origin   Target

Under-shot   Over-shot

5 Bracketing exercises

                                            B

Point of Origin:——>>>under-shot—-[*target*]—-over-shot>>>

                    A

Identify

(A)   the under-shot action as opposed to

(B)   the over-shot activity in hitting the target.

In normal collective bargaining negotiations between
      _____labor and
      _____management over a new contract.

In satisfying consumer demand for goods,
      ____a price driven free marketplace versus
      ____an economy centrally planned.

In seeking peace among nations, the use of
      ____diplomacy and
      ____war.

As a toddler strives to walk
      _____but crawls, rises and
      _____then lunges and topples.

Progress according to the cliché consists of
      _____two steps backward, and
      _____one step forward.

Planning ahead involves
      _____scheduling events and
      _____having back-up plans for emergencies.

The principle of the "Hiding Hand"
      _____in the first stage of a project
      _____in the latter stages.

6 Convergent/Divergent Forces

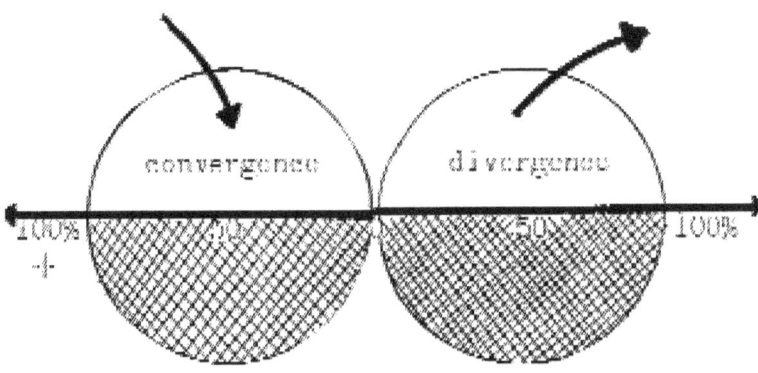

E Pluribus Unum?

6 Convergent/Divergent Social Forces exercises

Our National Motto is E Pluribus Unum, diversity within unity. All societies have ideas, actions, processes, events, and other large social changes that create tensions as they divide and unite society at times simultaneously.

In the following examples initially assign a + or—to what you think each of these ideas, products, events and social roles does to our society.

Then go over each choice and assign (0 to 100%) weight to each + or -.

Can some of these items have both positive and negative effects at the same time? Indicate with an asterisk.

_____the automobile_____

_____television_____

_____common language_____

_____street crime_____

_____schools_____

_____pro-sports_____

_____government_____

_____movies_____

_____home computer_____

_____traditions_____

_____spray paint can_____

_____the jet plane_____

(+)   _____drugs_____   (-)

_____floods, fires,_____

tornadoes, etc._____

_____boom boxes_____

_____racism_____

_____AIDS_____

_____marketplace_____

_____government "red tape"

_____the family_____

_____religion_____

_____child abuse_____

_____lawyers_____

_____doctors_____

_____nurses_____

_____teachers_____

_____clergy_____

_____scientists_____

_____engineers_____

_____corporate mgrs._____

_____hippie culture_____

_____hand guns_____

_____city smog_____

_____polluted beaches_____

_____acid rain_____

7. Whole/Part Relationships

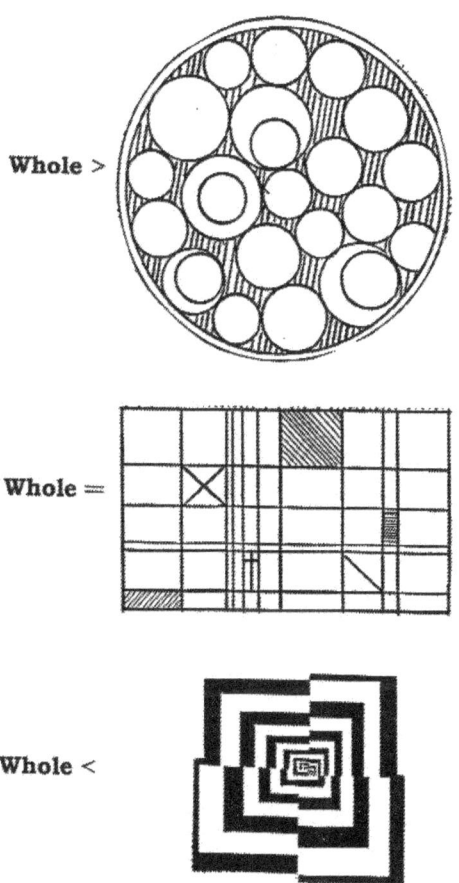

Whole >

Whole =

Whole <

7 Whole/Parts Relationships exercises

Of the following, identify which of the three conditions:
A, B, or C best applies to each example.

A   Whole = sum of the parts
B   Whole > sum of the parts
C   Whole < sum of the parts

_____Run on bank deposits during the 1930s.
_____Society as a compact of the dead, living and posterity.
_____Announcement of food rationing leading to shortages.
_____Public knowledge.
_____Black plague in Europe during 14th Century.
_____Year one, pennant winning team putting out 110% effort.
_____Year two, the same team came in third in the standings.
_____A corpse.
_____Corporate conglomerate selling off unrelated sub-units.
_____A new car @ $20,000.
_____The same car chopped up and parts sold for $50,000.
_____A live person.
_____Common language.
_____Lifeboat triage.

8 Sidling/Parallel Concept

Learning by "sidling along" or by overlapping;
another variant is "one step forward, two steps backward."

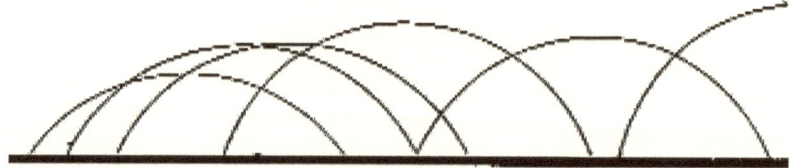

8 Sidling/Parallel Effect exercises

Fill in the corresponding, parallel or overlapping idea, product, practice or system that temporarily or permanently *co-exists with it*.

* electric light   _____
* Salk polio vaccine   _____
* equal opportunity   _____
* Beta VCR   _____

* steam locomotive   _____
* handicrafts   _____
* sailing ships   _____
* propeller airplanes   _____
* black/white TV   _____
* government   _____
* US   _____
* folk medicine   _____
* federal government   _____
* nuclear power   _____
* life   _____
* cable pay TV   _____
* 33rpm vinyl records   _____
* social order   _____
* astrology   _____
* love   _____
* ignorance   _____
* foresight   _____
* dish washer   _____
* aspirin (Bayer)   _____
* gasoline engine   _____
* analog audio tapes   _____
* immigrants:
  old language   _____
* ATM machine   _____
* direct current   _____
* CD recording   _____
* microwave oven   _____
* cellular phone   _____
* fluorescent light   _____
* Chinese acupuncture   _____
* Thomas Edison   _____

* ATM machine   _____
* popular culture   _____

9. Value, added Spectrum

[From *raw* materials to finished products, from information to meaning and knowledge.]

What Who When	today's/yesterday's/ news		news	analysis/opinions	=	meaning/ action
						»»»»»»

??? Where How many How much Why	spot	+	update	+	context	+	conclusions=meaning - (*jumping to* *conclusions*)
	1		2		3		4

5

What					
Who	**today's/yesterday's/analysis/opinion = meaning/**				
When	**news**	**news**			**action**

_____>>>>>>>

???

Where					
How many	**spot +**	**update +**	**context +**	**conclusions=meaning**	
How much				**—(*jumping to***	
Why				***conclusions*)**	
	1	**2**	**3**	**4**	**5**

9 Value-added Spectrum exercises

Complete the spectrum with the missing step. Do not use transportation as it has been subsumed by the following stage or step.

1. iron ore/smelter/_____/sheet steel/automobile
   /new car dealer/consumer
2. seed/wheat/harvest/silo/_____/store/bread/sale
3. seed/cotton/harvest/_____/garment shops/dept.
   stores /broadcloth/shirts, sheets, etc.
4. unskilled worker/_____/experience/supervision
   /competence/higher pay/better job elsewhere
5. pre-natal care/training/_____/experience/
   second baby/etc.
6. pre-school/high school diploma/ B.A.,_____,M.BA.
   /M.D., Ph.D., LL.D./higher incomes
7. simple/jack-of-all-trades/_____/complex
8. seedlings/trees/logs/_____/plywood/houses/
   furniture stores/misc., baseball bats, etc.
9. food/warehouse/_____/consumer choice
10. primitive existence/_____/cash crop/wider market
    /advanced economy
11. oral tradition/printing/mail/photography/telegraph/
    /_____/movies/radio/(transistor)/television/telex/
    /   /(micro-chip)/_____/satellites/fax
    machines/Internet
12. walking/horseback/stagecoach/_____/trolley/bicycle/car/
    bus/_____(water transit excluded)

10 Playing the Game

Figure 1

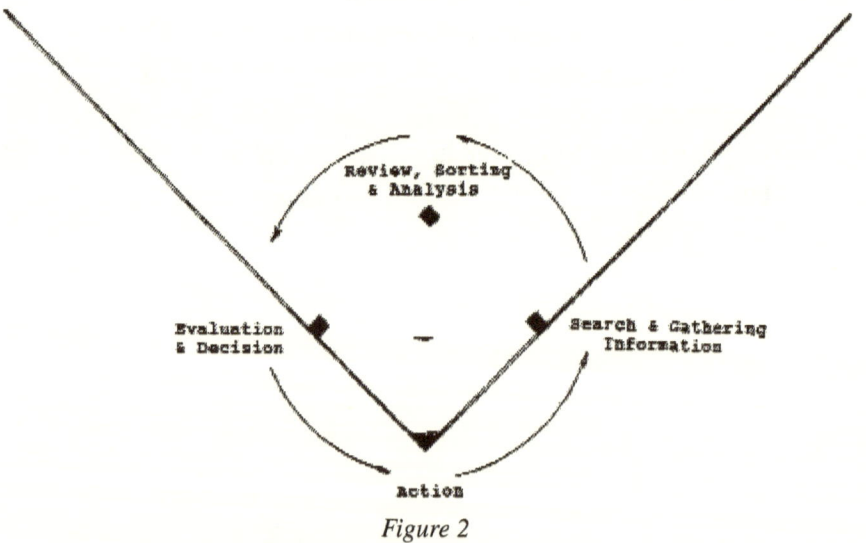

Figure 2

"Playing" the Game of Problem Solving:

In terms of the baseball diamond, Figure 1 represents an attempt to "play" the game *how?*

_____

_____

_____.

Similarly, Figure 2 tells us *what* about the Senator's frame of mind and of legislative making in general?

_____

_____

_____

_____.

Lastly, what does the phrase *"cutting the cloth to fit"* the facts, mean in terms of "playing" the game of problem solving?

_____

_____

_____

_____.

Part Two

Mental Applications And Exercises

3 Into the Problem Pits!

In this chapter current public issues and thought problems await our pastime. What are the payoffs? After applying the tools of the foregoing chapters, whether individually or by teamwork, the "problems" will lend themselves if not to "solutions" then at least to new understandings. *[Alternately, the reader may wish to peruse as background Part Three before proceeding further.]*

Thus, we introduce a set of social problems with attendant questions for further inquiry whether by library or field research. Of course, some of the problems may be sub-divided and repackaged, or postponed, or used as springboards for issues of your choosing.

This list does not exhaust the supply of issues that require more than glib opinions casually acquired from street banter or from media editorials. The alternative to overcooked opinions (and often yesterday's cluster of mistakes) is active problem solving. To begin,

>>1.   What is the "Greenhouse Effect"?
    a). is the evidence clear? contradictory?
    b). do experts agree or disagree?
      by degree or in kind?
    c). what is the cause(s)?
    d). what solutions have been proposed?
    e). are the solutions feasible? and solved
      by existing, or new, technology?

who will pay? private or public funds?

>>2.   What is the Gaia Hypothesis?
  a). does the hypothesis confirm or challenge
  the "Greenhouse Effect"?
  b). when scientists disagree over the effects of "global warning,"
  how does one determine the truth of the matter? by scientific
  testing and new evidence? by majority rule of the legislature? by
  a judicial decision? by public opinion polls?

>>3.   Do we need a national energy policy?
  a). should the federal government or the marketplace determine the
  energy use of business, consumers and government?
  b). what is "wrong" with importing oil? is it equally "wrong" to
  import coffee, bananas, tin, diamonds, copper and other basic
  and finished goods?
  c). is the call for a national energy policy by the federal government
  a "ploy" to get most Americans to give up their automobiles in
  favor of public transit?

>>4.   After the OPEC embargo in the early 1970s, a number of
  groups domestically and internationally predicted that the supply of petroleum would dwindle rapidly.
  a). on what assumptions and information did the Club of Rome and
  other groups predict the disappearance of petroleum?
  b). if the supply of petroleum was dwindling why did the price of a
  barrel of oil plunge in the 1980s?
  c). what assumptions went wrong? what facts did not materialize
  with their predictions?
  d). what other global forecasts of doom have gone awry? Why?
  e). why has the price of oil jumped in 2000?

>>5.   Thomas Malthus in 1798 postulated that since the number of
  people born each year grew geometrically while the supply of

food grew arithmetically, the result would be poverty and starvation. What went wrong with this grim prediction?

>>6.   The Federal farm programs

1. since the 1930s various federal programs have sought to help the American farmer: which crops are singled out for assistance?

2. what form does this assistance take?

a). landbank/crop reduction?

b). price support/storage?

c). marketing orders: oranges?

d). agricultural research

e). what has been the total cost of taxes and higher prices to the citizen and consumer since the 1930s?

f). do the programs work? for whom?

g). without government support of crop prices, will all farmers go bankrupt?

h). what is the futures market? why don't farmers use it individually or through cooperatives to hedge the prices of their commodities against volatile swings?

>>7.   In the 1920s, Brazil and Argentina were seen as entering the ranks of developed nations with high per capita income.

a). what went wrong with both countries?

i. historical factors?

ii. institutional resistance to change?

iii. political and military diversions?

iv. overly generous welfare state benefits and subsidies to business?

v. what is *capital flight*? why does it take place?

vi. is hyper-inflation over time in both countries the *cause or consequence* of the above factors?

>>8.   The homeless in America

a). who are the homeless by age, sex, and work experience?

b). how many are homeless? how reliable are the figures?

c). what is the turnover of the homeless? how many remain homeless longer than a year?

d). what is the composition of the homeless?

    i. children under 16

    ii. alcohol and drug addicts

    iii. mentally disturbed individuals released from institutions since the 1960s

    iv. criminals

    v. males under 25

    vi. why have governmental programs and benefits such as welfare, food stamps, free school lunches, Medicaid, and public housing along with the efforts of community based agencies not "solved" this issue?

    vii. what effect has *rent control* by local governments in New York City, Berkeley and elsewhere had on the homeless in terms of finding low cost housing?

    (In the above questions there is some overlapping.)

>>9.   Police/traffic control

a). why have the police been given the job of traffic control? for historical reasons? by default?

b). why do police issue traffic tickets for speed violations, parking violations and for pedestrian jay walking? to stop such behaviors? or to raise revenues?

c). is the purpose of traffic control to punish drivers or to expedite traffic flows and safety?

d). in what way is the issuing of traffic tickets different from installing traffic lights (zero-sum), paint lane dividers, directional signs, and four-way stop signs (negative-sum)?

e). are there public or private agencies that hold yearly conferences on how to *improve traffic flows,* or how to *improve the safety of the motoring public and pedestrians*? If no conferences are held on these topics, why not?

f). why do local and state traffic agencies install traffic lights, two-way stop signs, and four-way stop signs as if they were inter-changeable substitutes?

g). why are not street lights lowered along heavily used streets to shed more illumination? reduce crime?

h). what other practices do local and state traffic agencies engage in that foster discourtesy and danger to the motoring public?

i). what percentage of the annual city and state police budgets is spent on *basic research* whether it be for crime control or traffic control?

>>10. Over the last century what has happened to the stability of the family in the United States and Western Europe?

a). what has happened to the marriage rate over this period? the divorce rate? the rate of children born out of wedlock?

b). what ideas and attitudes have affected family formation?

c). what effects has the availability of contraceptive devices had on the family?

d). has the rearing of children changed in this time period? have schools served to support or challenge the central role of the family?

e) what circumstances have diminished parental authority?

f) how have the media and Hollywood portrayed the family and the rearing of children?

>>11. What effects has "talking trash" the graffiti of language had on families, communities and society?

a). why have four letter words formerly considered obscene and in bad taste so common now?

b). what effects have the movies had in spreading the talking of trash?

c). what effects have TV talk shows had on what topics to discuss that were formerly considered unsuitable?

d). are there connections between visual and verbal pollutions on behavior?

e) what is the purpose of codes of etiquette and manners?

f). who gains and who loses when anything can be said, anything done, and anything goes?

>>12.   What does *price fixing* by government achieve?
Who gains? Who loses? What permanent
market distortions take place in our economy?

a). who gains when milk, peanuts and other agricultural prices are *fixed above* the market price?

b). who gains when rent controls on apartments are fixed *below* the market price?

c). who gains when loans are fixed or mandated at interest rates *below* the market price?

d). who gains with a fixed minimum wage?

e). who loses in each of the above cases?

f). why is it that fixing prices in the marketplace is subject to the *anti-monopoly laws such as the Sherman and Clayton acts*, but when the federal or state governments engage in price fixing, the laws are not applied?

>>13.   What is the NIMBY (Not-in-My-Backyard) Syndrome?

a). what is an environmental impact study? are such studies easy or difficult to compile? what skills and training are required for this task?

b). does the NIMBY protest apply solely to public or governmental actions? to marketplace actions as well?

c). does economic growth and land development come under a or b?

d). if many NIMBY protests are successful what effects will it have on our economy and society? in the near-term and long-term future?

>>14.   If the United States dissolved into fifty separate nations each with its own defense departments, currencies, border controls, customs and tariffs, passports, etc.

a). what effects would it have on the standard of living of different regions and states?

b). what effects would the split-up have on peaceful relations among the fifty states?

c). what effects would the dissolution have on foreign events? How would Canada and Mexico respond to the breakup of the United States?

>>15. If the United States adopted a national health program such as Great Britain's in which every American would have access to medical care at no cost, but totally federally [taxpayer] funded what would be the effects:

a). on the various medical indices of health:
      infant mortality, aging, cancer, etc.?

b). what effect would it have on attracting talented people into the medical branches?

c). what effect would this new program have on the federal budget deficit?

d). what would be the long term effects on medical innovation of drugs, technology, new procedures, etc.?

e). what percentage of GNP do we currently spend on health care? Will it increase or decrease after a national health program is inaugurated?

f). how much did the health plan of the Clinton administration resemble the single-payer plan of Great Britain's?

g). in countries that have adopted national health programs such as Canada, Sweden and the Netherlands, apply questions a through f above.

>>16. Why have certain diseases re-appeared in our time?
A tuberculosis B pneumonia C cholera

a). because of genetic or environmental factors?

b). because of biological factors?

c). because of poverty?

Finally, what are the limits of social problem solving? More often than not, problem solving is likely to succeed if the issue is quantifiable, that is, if we can ask how many, how much, how long, etc. Secondly if the facts to the preceding questions can be ascertained, at some reasonable cost and time, so much the better. But if a public issue involves tastes and attitudes: that is, the willingness by individuals to use drugs and alcohol deliberately and to excess, then even if quantifiable, the issue does not lend itself to a simple solution as we have discovered as a society. Our endless wars on poverty, cancer, crime, drugs and guns may suggest, at least that the war metaphor is not apt for identifying or solving social issues.

Thirdly, neither the federal government nor any other public or private agency has a magic wand to wish away any issue. If public attitudes grow and form a climate of opinion opposed to the law as in Prohibition during the 1920s, then the instrument of the law will be diminished.

Lastly, if problems are not dealt early-on then they may escalate out of frustration into public conflicts. In turn, violence may ensue as a by product and become a perennial issue as the Hatfield and McCoy feuds illustrate, or as strife for a generation in Northern Ireland runs on, and as ethnic and tribal cleansing in the former Yugoslavia and Rwanda has illustrated.

4 What If...?

Thomas Jefferson spoke of a crusade against ignorance. He was concerned that democracy could thrive only if its citizens were truly informed. Hence his unabashed support for public education. But along with the schools, the media has a vital collateral task in a democracy to provide not just entertainment and junk-food news, but information that is current, in context and sheds light on the non-profit sector, the marketplace and the workings of government. Without this *civic wallpaper of reality*, the citizenry can only grope in the wilderness of half-truths, trivia, lies and misinformation.

What follows then are a series of *"what if"* scenarios as they might affect the media, government, education and the environment. As mind-benders, they are meant to be suggestive. As such they continue the mental gymnastics begun earlier. By raising these thought experiments we seek to provide a direction for further discussion, inquiry, and exploration. Perhaps, as a result, the future may have fewer surprises in store for us. And fewer mistakes to stumble over. To begin with:

* What if the newscasts of the *ABC, CBS, NBC, CNN* networks and the PBS Lehrer hour dispensed with the faces of the reporters and anchors in favor of voice-overs *only*. (By contrast in the press today we get either the reporter's by-line at the top of the story, or the name of the news agency supplying the item, or an anonymous *staff reporter*.) Will the quality of reporting improve or decline?

* What if the major newspapers across the land on Sundays issued their own equivalent to the *New York Times* Sunday "News of the Week in Review?"

* What if again the major newspapers assigned a cadre of investigative reporters to pursue local, state, national and international topics *throughout* the year?

* What if television news departments did the same? The networks could revive the hour-long documentary and use it a second time by inserting the documentary into five-minute reports on the nightly news so that the investigative work could gain double exposure? (After all the instant replay in sporting events, permits the replaying of the same play over and over until it sinks in.) Why not the "plays" of the public?

* What if newspapers and television news began to present foreign and military aid within a context so that the ordinary citizen would gain some sense of what these billions of dollars have achieved since 1947 for the American people as well as for the recipient nations?

* What if in addition to the Dow Jones Index figure nightly, the media would announce the daily federal budget deficit/surplus figures? Would it be a misleading figure? Would we have a better sense of what the federal government is doing day by day? What else would we need to know?

* What if the press could itemize and identify the senators and representatives who *sponsored new programs* and/or additions to existing programs as well as the legislators who proposed *abolishing existing programs* that had outlived their usefulness?

* What if governmental budgets of all programs on the local, state and federal levels were subjected to *sunset laws of five years*? Why in fact are governmental budget on all levels simply allowed to grow without serious budgetary scrutiny and control?

* What if a constitutional amendment limited representatives and senators to two terms? (Why is the first law of politics: to get elected;

the second, to get re-elected?, and third, to stay elected? How does this attitude and stance by politicians serve the public?)

* What if the Congress when it passed the National Highway Defense Act in 1956 creating the interstate freeway system, had created also a an *east/west six lane toll expressway solely for trucks* running on a rough diagonal from New York City to Chicago to Los Angeles? What would be different today? On transportation costs? On the railroads?

* What if the Congress in order to achieve clear air and water for the country compelled all business firms, local governments and non-profit agencies to return to the office, plant, store, hospital, school and college *size and technologies* of 1905? What would happen to the standard of living?

* What if the Congress had mandated in the 1950s as Canada and France did that only *one type or model* of nuclear reactor could be constructed by utilities throughout the country? Would there be more or fewer nuclear plants today?

* What if all public airports were auctioned-off to private bidders throughout the land? Would consumers benefit? By price and service?

* What if the Congress passed a law permitting either AT & T or IBM to operate the air-controller system on five year renewable contracts? Would the skies be safer for travelers? At lower or higher costs?

* What if the Congress permitted all new workers entering the future labor force to either join the Social Security system or to place the combined amount of individual contribution and employer payroll taxes into an Individual Retirement Account (IRA)? What would be the effects of this proposal on labor mobility? On private investments? On economic growth? On the scope and power of the federal government?

* What if a private national computer bank of job openings came into existence? Would unemployment drop? Would the unemployed move? For shorter or longer distances? How did unemployment plunge sharply in the 1990s without a national computer bank of jobs openings?

* What if graffiti vanished from the surfaces of schools, parks, buildings, homes, subway cars, buses, abandoned homes, bridges? Or is vandalism simply another sign of urban decay to be accepted as a fact of life?

* What if all four-way stop signs were replaced either by two-way signs or a regular traffic light across the land? What beneficial effects would flow from this change? Harmful ones?

* What if the Cold War between the Soviet Union and the West is truly over? But will Russia challenge or resume its anti-Western stance? Will conflicts erupt elsewhere in the world unexpectedly?

* * *

Finally, what if *most, some,* or even a *few* of the above "what if" scenarios came to pass? What impact would these changes singly and together have on the media, government, business, education and society? What difference would it make to the quality of life for individuals and families in our society? Who would be the winners? the losers? What other consequences would flow from these changes?

Lastly, driven by mistakes and errors, the requisite array of problem solving skills emerges for young and old at home, at school, and in the world of work. In this voyage of discovery, the mind is free to search for the new, to connect the old and new, and to transform the myriad disconnected pieces of the puzzle of human experiences into knowledge.

Part Three

Mental Wallpapers

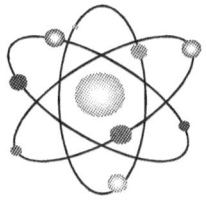

5 What is the Problem?

How do we go about solving our daily problems? As to the basics of food, shelter, clothing and affection, infants are helpless but not completely so as to making their wishes known. Quickly the infant announces the need for nourishment and diaper changes by gurgles, groans, whimpers or several screams. Parents, too, learn by trial and error to distinguish which signals to pay heed. For the most part, our introduction to problem solving (personal and family) began at our parental knees as they whispered, read or sang us to sleep. From these stories one learned how to be patient, to achieve, and to live with others. From our parents we received affection and daily encouragement as well as their shining example.

As the toddler left the love and blandishments of parents for preschool, a new setting provided an opportunity to test then and later the ways and means of getting along with other youngsters by pulling, hitting, hugging, shoving, smiling and speaking. As to the new adults about us they took some getting used to. Not all adults were stand-ins for mothers and father. By adolescence much would be internalized, but not all as facial gestures, posture, speech, clothing and appearance revealed much about us. With physical growth and the pumping of hormones, new desires emerged.

From childhood to adolescence, some children learn to use temper tantrums, tears, aloofness and other emotional tactics or "tricks" to solve their pressing wishes. While other children unable to deal with cruelty or abuse in the family, leave. Still others learn to act as incipient adults by consideration and courtesy to others. Some follow parental clues and achieve in school. For the fortunate, rewards follow such as the use of the family car, personal phone, credit cards, ski and vacation trips. But for children who did poorly in school their future options may shrink unless social programs offset various handicaps.

To a toddler, wishes, needs and necessities are all one buzzing desire. Of course the child's needs or wants may be at variance with parental values and family income. In fortunate homes, the child may assume that he or she is at the center of the universe to command others. That is unless challenged by siblings, friends and relatives.

So the concentric circle of infancy with material needs gives way gradually to the second circle of affection, and warmth and love to be followed by the third circle of adolescence with the rebirth of personality and on to the fourth circle of taking one's place in school, community, on the job and in society.

For the most part, the foregoing means of tackling personal problems are *informal* ways, but gradually by high school and college, the ways turn more *formal* and elaborate until the adolescent reaches the age of majority. Then laws, rules and contracts become guiding principles and shape solutions to daily issues of home and workplace.

We live in age of rules, seemingly endless choices and buzzing information. Therefore the first step is to reduce risk, uncertainty and complexity. The key to an orderly life is the reduction of countless decisions to *habit and routine*. Then one is free to deal with novelty and the exceptions, both minor and major that come along. How?

Problem solving involves active personal involvement by first asking *what is the problem*, secondly what *information do you need to know*, thirdly is *expert advice available* and affordable, next, what are the *money constraints* and *options*, and finally what, where and when are the *payoffs*? Or we may seek to obtain "canned" information that involves the experience of others in using, let us say, an appliance or automobile. Or we may prefer the for-hire testimony of experts who have conducted tests on various products. We are then free to evaluate this information or to disregard it as we make choices in the marketplace.

A key problem solving avenue of reducing risk to routine is by the purchase of insurance in its many guises of life, auto, fire, home, health, accident, and travel. This does not diminish the need for prudence by individuals and families for rainy-day savings whether for unemployment, major medical bills, vacation, retirement and unforeseen events.

To be sure, the ability to choose from a menu of insurance strategies demands a suitable income, education, and willingness to survey, compare, and choose the appropriate insurance scheme that reduces risk and increases security and freedom.

However when individual problem solving is unable to handle uncertainty and risk, a turn to societal solution may be in order. For example, there are certain events such as unemployment that have been turned into social obligations serviced by the federal government. Finally when other events such as acts of God involve heavy financial losses to property as a result of hurricanes, floods, tornadoes and earthquakes, the losses have been for the most part (aside from private insurance) socialized in the form of cash subsidies and low cost federal loans for recovery and rebuilding.

Some would argue that as the extent and range of social security grows; the need for individual rainy-day savings becomes less necessary. Thus over time a society-wide problem solving method *substitutes* at least in part for individual problem solving and decision.

Generally we reduce many choices of daily life to habit and routine by trial and error. Thus mistakes and errors lead to problem solving. Furthermore, at the parental knee, the toddler, for example, may be prepared for college by daily reminders of the future road to be taken. On the other hand, many daily decisions, for example, involve brands of toothpaste, gasoline, beer, and breakfast cereal that are of minor matters. But others such as the choice of residence, job, spouse, religion and political candidates involve matters of substance that are no less the product of habit and routine.

What are the limits of personal problem solving? In using the experience of friends and others, there are several limitations involving "fish-story" exaggeration, the hiding of disagreeable information lest one admit a mistake, and the inability to separate the exception from typical results. However when we turn to experts, the foregoing limitations of *evidence and context* are controlled or reduced. Unless experts choose, that is, to puff their knowledge with the use of jargon. Beyond puffery lies the quack "experts" using phony credentials.

Why is there a need for experts? Partly due to the explosion of knowledge and information flows. Also many individuals lack the time to pursue economic and political events or to do their nightly civic homework. Thus when individuals, institutions and society require problem solving beyond the simple rules of routine and common sense, the expertise of specialists is sought. For the individual needing a will, contract, or divorce, the skills of attorneys are invariably necessary.

More familiarly, when we are ill, we turn usually to doctors and to further specialists in hospitals. But for others who harbor distrust of traditional medicine, there are alternatives in prayer, folk medicine and acupuncture.

When serious illness strikes a member of the family, there are often community support groups that provide emotional comfort and basic answers as to what to expect, what to do and where to seek other help in ministering to the needs of the loved one as well as the family under siege. The support groups provide a form of expert advice gained from hard-won experiences.

Turning to material matters, the home is another area requiring often the services of specialist whether it is a plumber, electrician, or appliance and furnace repairman. After the home, the automobile requires the skills of trained mechanics. Do-it-your-selfers and tinkerers can perform some tasks at home and on the car, but there are *limits*. Without training and the proper tools for the weekend tinkerer, costly disaster may lurk in the offing.

When a product appears defective due to negligence, there is an entire industry of special lawyers ready and willing to launch a single or class action suit.

Of course, business firms also require expert advice in the form of marketing surveys as to whether a new location of store or plant is necessary; or market research as to whether a new product will be favorably received; finally, some large corporations hire consulting firms to "discover" what the corporate board wished to do all along whether it was the sell-off of certain product lines, closure of plants, mergers, etc.

But it has been government at all levels that has sought the help of outside experts to propose solutions to pressing political, economic, medical and technical problems. On the federal level, a favorite technique has been to appoint Presidential Commissions and Congressional research agencies to tackle specific issues:

Political: What caused the riots of the 1960s? Who assassinated President Kennedy?

Economic: Will the N.A.F.T.A. agreement among the U.S., Canada and Mexico be good for all three nations? Should free trade be extended to the European Union nations?

Technical: Should the federal government fund private research and development?

Medical: Will additional federal funds be sufficient to obtain cures for many deadly diseases?

Financial: How should social security be funded? Should private IRAs be expanded to replace social security?

Agriculture: do the various farm subsidies since 1934 help to sustain farm income? At what cost to the taxpayer and the consumer?

As noted the US Congress has its own in-house experts: the General Accounting Office (GAO), Congressional Budget Office (CBO), and Congressional Research Service (CRS) to perform research on the above and other topics. Aside from in-house government research agencies, the alternative is to commission the "Beltway Institutions" of the nation's capital and elsewhere: universities, think tanks, and consulting firms to provide expert advice on a wide range of problems and issues.

How does one become an expert? The dictionary informs us that an expert is a person with a high degree of skill in, or knowledge of a certain subject. Sometimes governmental permission to practice is essential. After having studied and passed state examinations, doctors and lawyers are then licensed to practice. Presumably the public is protected from quack practitioners in this manner.

On the other hand, scientists from physicists to biologists and mathematicians are trained and certified by degrees from reputable institutions of higher learning. But that is only the first step. More importantly those who add to the stock of new knowledge by publishing new findings are then subject to peer review. But the ultimate check on quackery in science is the ability of others to replicate the findings in the laboratory, or on the chalkboard, or by computer. But certainly not by majority rule of ordinary citizens or legislative majorities. Majority rule has very little to do with new knowledge and truth.

Scientists who disagree over some aspects of their chosen field is one matter, but scientists who disagree over politics, foreign policy, military weapons, nuclear energy, the homeless, abortion, the mentally ill and other public issues merit no deference for their political opinions. Not surprisingly scientists can be as emotional, ignorant, duped by charlatans and make unwise recommendations on public issues as anyone else.

What then is the difference between experts who disagree and layman who disagree over the *same* topic? Presumably over the range of disagreement. If experts on politics do not differ more narrowly than the public, then experts appear as so many "guns for hire" to push one side of the story.

Yet experts of all stripes insist that they apply some *systematic method of fact* finding to the collecting and sifting of information as well as the use of *a framework or context* before deciding, or making recommendations.

For example, of lawyers licensed today 90% never enter the court-room for trial by combat. Thus lawyerly skills involve knowledge of the law, a method of reasoning, organizing skills, etc. Hence in their view, law school skills may be applied to private and public matters, business and governmental issues.

As to scholars such as historians, literary critics, biographers, journalists, etc. they are engaged in the search for facts, patterns, distinctions, causes and consequences, meaning, etc. Like lawyers they too bring a systematic approach to their searches.

Similarly social scientists that include economists, sociologists, anthropologists, political scientists and others aspire to the breadth and precision that the natural scientists practice. They too are practitioners of methods but the social sciences can not conduct tests on human beings as biologists can nor are their results replicated in the four corners of the world. For one, information is often incomplete. Also cultural considerations color, unwittingly the results and conclusions of social research.

On the other hand, the natural scientists of our age with their jargon, mathematics, and assortment of linear accelerators, lasers, computers, atom smashers and other tools appear to be the new high priests of our age. Also a bit beyond us, seeing further or deeper into reality. As men and women in "white coats," they appear to be detached until such time as they pronounce on political issues. They then reveal their human failings like the rest of us.

Yet Mother Nature, the playpen of scientists may offer us the newest tools in problem solving. As one writer observed, "Companies and scientists are turning to a wide variety of natural models—from the way salmon migrate to how the human body fights viruses to evolution—for new approaches to problem solving."

In a nutshell, problem solving may be initiated and resolved on various levels separately or concurrently by the individual in the home, by insurance companies, by other market purchases, or by various levels of government collectively.

In addition problem solving takes place on a *continuum of expanding circles* of number, complexity, recurrence, cost, and feasibility. The actors in this drama range from the individual through groups to institutions such as non-profit agencies, business firms and governmental agencies.

But the *shape* of problem solving provides still another perspective. Problems may be classified as simple and hard. For example, sorting a deck of cards by suits is fairly simple. But sorting a thousand piece jigsaw puzzle is not so. Also problems vary by length of *time* involved, some require blocks of time serially, but others gobble time up exponentially. [An example of the latter rate is the Malthusian hypothesis that while the supply of food grows arithmetically (1,2,3,4, etc.) the population of the economy or the globe grows geometrically (1,2,4,8,16,32, etc.].

Finally mathematicians immersed in complexity theory argue that hard problems are easy to verify once completed as in the jigsaw puzzle that requires a few seconds to see if you have it right.

On the other hand simple problems may have many details but lack focus as to fit, coherence, meaning, and solution. For example, at the scene of head-on car collisions, bodies may be strewn about; some bloodied, some in shock, some in audible pain, etc. Aside from first aid, the decision to move the victims should be made by professionals:

para-medics, nurses, and physicians. They must make separate diagnoses, render further medical assistance and seek additional or standby help. The second order function often performed by the police is to determine the cause(s) of the accident. Evidence must be gathered, events reconstructed, technical and lab tests performed and then conclusions drawn. In brief, while problem solving is as normal as breathing, some individuals may choose not to play the game as it demands curiosity, diligence, time and sustained thought.

6 Which One to Buy, When, Where?

In the marketplace in America, the consumer is king. No matter in what shopping mall, store, warehouse, or emporium, the consumer visits, shops, and buys. He or she decides in a voluntary and selective manner what to buy, when, where, and how much to pay, as well as whether to pay cash or to use credit. The marketplace works quietly, efficiently, and offers countless choices to the sometime weary consumer. But the marketplace is nothing more than people willing to voluntarily *exchange* their labor and capital for goods and services. These millions of voluntary exchanges are made possible by the medium of money.

Aside from merchandise, equally available are services that run the gamut from the personal ones of grooming, and health to the services of others engaged in auto repairs, garden tending, domestic help, child care, tax and investment services, travel help and countless more services catering to consumers who wish to substitute money for time.

For most Americans, an economic system of *market prices* that draws forth the production and distribution of goods and services is simply *taken for granted*. That is, until one survives an earthquake or a hurricane as in South Florida in 1992 only to painfully discover that what one took for granted: running water, electricity, shelter and normal markets do not exist!

Or to visit foreign lands where many goods and services are price controlled in nearly empty stores with queues of consumers for scarce food items of poor quality. The former Soviet Union and Eastern European countries were shining examples of economic systems hostile to the consumer. But there are also many other countries with economies that work as poorly as in Cuba, North Korea, Albania and Russia.

With the consumer as the driving force, unsold goods in our economy are placed on sale and sold at a more attractive price. Again, this method of *clearing markets* is taken for granted. Not so in the former Soviet Union where unsold goods gathered dust and mold in warehouses. Thus the most important aspect of a price directed marketplace is to *reduce mistakes and errors* of over-production to manageable and routine problem solving by running sales.

On the other hand, in an economy directed from the nation's capital, where all the means of production are government owned, where all employees are government employees, there is *no incentive* to correct production mistakes and errors of quantity and quality. Thus centrally controlled economies waste both human resources and scarce materials in countless ways. Aside from gathering dust, the unwanted goods each year could (except for ecological considerations) just as well be burned or taken out to sea for burial. Or simply allowed to decay. In short government bureaucrats are allowed to "produce" *unlimited mistakes* while consumers watch as the mistakes turn into endless shortages of shoddy goods and services.

But *normal (or white)* markets can be disturbed as a result of an earthquake or hurricane when temporary *gray markets* can appear for bottled water, camping stoves and lamps, cellular phones, and other goods in demand. Too often the first reaction is to denounce the higher prices as gouging. The charge is misguided. Would people be better off if no one took the initiative to buy, transport and set up a stand for these desirable goods? These are often brand names of known quality at temporarily higher price.

After World War II, there were *gray markets* for a few years since demand exceeded the supplies in our economy for many durable civilian goods such as automobiles and home appliances. As a result, there were long waiting lists for these goods. Some consumers in order to move from the bottom to the top of these waiting lists passed cash bribes under the table to the dealers. But as production increased and consumers were supplied these gray markets vanished.

Also in economies with market driven prices or centrally controlled, *black markets* may appear over the sale of prohibited goods such as drugs, weapons, exchange of currencies, gambling and other vices. The pervasive problems with black market goods are their unknown sources, quality, and higher prices to cover the costs of detection and likely imprisonment.

However black markets may also arise as during World War II in our economy when coupons rationed goods such as gasoline, sugar, meat and other items. In addition price controls were imposed as well. Since the war years were prosperous domestically, consumers had money to pay black market prices for the above-mentioned goods even if it were illegal.

Putting aside black and gray markets, we return to the workings of a normal market economy. While an economy of prices and private property delivers the cornucopia of goods, individual business firms seek to reduce their fluctuations of sales by calling in the experts of Madison Avenue to mold consumer decisions to ones of habit. Thanks to the ubiquitous presence of ads everywhere, we all recognize the games of persuasion that may coincide with our own preference of choice and problem solving. The trick for the hucksters of persuasion is to make our preferences and the makers of brand X coincide.

Poor nations rarely require the services of advertisers. Those without income do not need advice on how to spend. But affluence and advertising go hand in hand. More often than not, advertising rides on the wave of economic growth and its resultant increases in material well-being. Yet economists for the most part take a dim view of the role of advertising. They do so not out of pique but rather from the perspective that advertisers are engaged in a shell game of selling more of one good at the expense of another seller. In short, GM's loss is, Ford's gain, or the decline of domestic auto sales may be offset by increased imports.

Economists concede that when advertising *informs* rather than *persuades* it provides a useful function for consumers. By providing information, consumers can act intelligently or more rationally. What type of ad would fit this bill? We are all familiar with the weekly food specials and variety store ads that list specials by price and number. These ads perform a clear function for the consumer in conserving time by announcing where the goods are, at what price, and when they are available.

However advertising agencies and their clients have long ignored this distinction. Why? Because in our affluent society, many final consumer goods and services are so *similar* as to be indistinguishable. Thus the appointed task of modern advertising is to sell goods by indirection, less on the merits, than of consumer emotional needs to be satisfied if brand x rather than brand y is purchased. As one advertiser noted that "You have to sell on emotion more than ever because it's a world of parity products out there." Parity is the euphemism for look-alike products. For the most part, the intrinsic qualities of televisions, VCRs, tires, tennis racquets, hair dryers and other appliances are non-existent to the consumer.

But consider, for example, jeans. If the same seamstress in Singapore is sewing on various labels, the price will vary according to the "designer labels" attached, but not to the garment itself. It is this realm of snob-appeal and symbolic add-on in higher prices that draws the ire of economists. Advertising raises the price of goods two ways, by the direct cost of advertising and the higher mark-up. Should economists object if consumers wish to be flimflammed? Moreover in a democracy and in a free marketplace, consumers have a right to pursue their own roads to happiness.

But economists are consistent. Along with their opposition to the unnecessary role of modern advertising, they object for similar reasons to gambling and lotteries in any guise or manner. For the losses of some, are the gains of others. As a result no *new* economic activity has been created, just a switch of funds from, say, Peter to Pauline. But surely Las Vegas and Atlantic City create jobs? Indeed, but these jobs are incidental to the transfer of funds from one party to another. To economists, the workers at these gambling places could be employed more productively elsewhere satisfying other consumer demands.

Despite these criticisms, advertising appears secure in its modern role of ticket taker. Advertising today moves on a few simple propositions about human nature. Initially, the consumer is assumed not to know the difference, if any, between and within categories of goods; secondly that the consumer will not consult consumer publications for ratings of goods and services; thirdly that the consumer is as likely to buy on impulse expensive durable goods, including homes, as inexpensive tooth paste; fourthly that despite consumer skepticism of ads in general, consumers will buy by brand name rather than generics. Given these assumptions, advertisers have a license to move consumers from one product queue to another.

Aside from dividing ads as to whether they inform or persuade, a still more useful distinction is between those messages that promise us an *exchange* versus those that *lecture* to us. The former asks the consumer to part with cash or credit in return for a product or service (or the voter is asked to vote for candidate X in exchange for his platform promises); or a citizen is asked to donate to a worthy cause in return for the glow of compassion. In these transactions an exchange of one kind or another takes place.

On the other hand, there are ads that hector or harangue us to *stop* certain personal behaviors: forest fires, littering, smoking, unsafe sex, the spread of AIDS, drug addiction and other public nuisances. Needless to say the latter group of public service ads are neither profitable nor as easily accomplished as selling breakfast cereals and soft drinks.

Then there are those institutional ads that offer neither a transaction nor a lecture, but are attempts to ingratiate the company, agency, or city, as a warm, caring, social or business firm. By indirection, the ads ask us to think well of Boeing, the Red Cross, the Big Apple, the United Way and Blue Cross. Then there are business firms that do not sell retail goods but are engaged in the production of intermediate or capital goods, yet they court public goodwill. These would include machine goods, steel companies and construction firms engaged in building industrial plants and factories. Thus they strive to implant their corporate logos into public consciousness. In fact, on public television, firms are restricted to showing their logos and mini-ads.

However as a crash course and introduction to our culture, the influence of advertising has not been given its due. With polyglot communities of newcomers to our shores, the old notion that the public schools would acculturate much less melt the new arrivals into main line Americans, must give way to the daily and tireless instructors on how Americans spend their money. But advertising agencies and their clients are not interested in claiming credit for this cultural spillover, a valuable social by-product.

Like robots, the televised commercials do not tire in their repetition. Why does modern advertising hammer away and repeat itself? For the consumer must not be permitted the luxury of recovering from the daily bombardment nor remained untouched. Above all, to take hold in the consumer's consciousness the ads require time. But technology grants the viewer the veto of the remote control. Today "zapping" TV ads appears increasingly pervasive.

Are those engaged in the arts of persuasion subject to basic limitations? Indeed they are despite the notion that the "black arts" of propaganda are but a step away from brainwashing. First of all, all forms of persuasion are likely to succeed it they go with the grain of existing tastes, attitudes, and preconceptions.

Secondly, the persuader whatever his kit bag of tricks cannot like King Canute hold back basic economic and social trends in the society. As Jacques Ellul a student of the subject observed, "Propaganda is definitely not an arsenal of ready-made valid techniques and arguments, suitable for use everywhere." Thirdly, persuasion builds its case on selective facts hurrying along to the ready-made conclusion: buy this product!

Lastly the persuasion must be continuous and lasting otherwise it melts away like an ice cube on a hot day. Subject to these limitations, and they are considerable, the persuaders hearken to their trade.

At this point we may also raise the question whether the efforts of advertising coincide with the wishes of individuals engaged in problem solving? As mentioned earlier, many purchases of goods are of little consequence whether we purchase a famous brand or the generic kind. The only question is whether we are led to buy or do things we do not wish to do against our true wishes.

The most compelling evidence that advertising does not have a blank check to treat us as willing slaves is the repetition daily of the same ad over and over. Apparently the daily booster shots do not take. Or we would likely see ads only once a month if the shots "took." This condition would suggest that we accept and reject most ads simultaneously, buying what we need, but rejecting the slick message.

A further word about altruism. In doing good for others, the citizen has a range of options as to how to proceed. He may simply purchase an array of "altruistic goods" much as he or she purchased private goods and services. That is, buying a certain amount, when and where desirable. For example, some may choose to tithe ten per cent of their income to their local church and its outreach programs in the immediate and wider community.

Or an individual may choose to make an annual contribution to the United Way. Or a variant of the preceding is to give to ad hoc groups that approach him on the street, at the shopping mall and at his residence for contributions.

Thus charitable contributions may be made to assist people (United Way), further research (American Heart Association) or foster political and environmental issues (Sierra Club).

Why should an individual buy "altruistic goods" of any variety? For one there is an impulse to do good, to feel good and the wish to be seen as dispensing goodness. Economists call the satisfaction received from these expenditures as "psychic income" as opposed to material satisfaction from typical goods and services. To induce individuals to donate, countless agencies devoted to the public interest offer a monthly magazine, membership card, and other tokens. Finally membership provides the agency with the means to discharge or espouse its goals.

The second avenue of assisting others is to donate one's time in soup kitchens, retirement homes, schools, churches, and other places. Or to aid some recovering alcoholic or drug addict. Thirdly one may canvass and solicit funds from others for various community agencies.

Or lastly one may choose to protest and demonstrate as a free lancer or as a recruit for the issue of the day. One is only a telephone away from some instant protest. These are calculated decisions. Finally, another realm involves spontaneous, Good Samaritan efforts during emergencies with no thought of reward.

In brief, one may engage in social problem solving by donating one's money, or time to one cause or another, thereby reaping psychic income for doing good.

7 Why Tax Me?

For the consumer, as we have seen, when he enters the marketplace the guiding principle is *the freedom to choose and select* given quantities of goods at tendered prices. When we turn to the realm of government as a problem solving institution, the principles are altered. With the consent of the governed, taxes are *compelled*, not voluntarily given. In turn the relatively few legislators, not by the millions of taxpayers, decide the amounts of taxes and government borrowings to cover budgetary expenditures and deficits.

What does one get for a tax dollar? Initially, given that the primary function of government is to provide for public order, hence taxes are exchanged for the public services of national defense, the police and fire departments. Secondly, other public services include the provision of water, sewers, garbage collection and schooling. Thirdly, even more directly some individuals and business firms receive monthly checks, or tax subsidies, or cheap loans and other government benefits. In the first two cases, the citizen/consumer receives a small portion of a collectively produced service. In the third case, *other* people receive cash and benefits from his and her taxes.

Generally governments have three means of assisting groups or the entire population of the nation. The federal government may grant special *tax subsidies* to farmers, merchant marine shippers, homeowners, and corporations; or it may *grant money* directly to farmers, to individual recipients of welfare checks and food stamps, or in the form of federal grants to states and local governments for specific programs such as education, crime fighting and medical care for indigents. Or it may *underwrite loans* to farmers, banks, big corporations (Chrysler, Lockheed), small businesses, homeowners, veterans, and college students.

What is the role of government in our lives? Over time, the federal and state governments have sought to *complement* and *supplement* the workings of the marketplace; to *redistribute income*; and to *counter the business cycle*. Once upon a time, Thomas Jefferson believed as a matter of principle that the government, which governed least, governed best. What role would fill Jefferson's principle? The first of the four modern roles for government.

Historically the government at all levels *complemented* the workings of the marketplace by the creation of roads, canals, and post office while encouraging the construction of the telegraph and railroads with land grants. Also the functions of national defense as well as the courts, prisons and police were seen as necessary to domestic peace. Hence, this role would be most recognizable by Jefferson if he were to revisit us on the eve of the twenty-first century.

The second role has been to *supplement* and temper the excesses of the marketplace. The recurrence and dislocations of unemployment, workplace injuries, illness and destitute old age, as noted earlier, have been assumed by government. The assumption has been that these by-products of the marketplace could not be rectified by individual prudence by purchasing individual insurance. Why? Given the ups-and downs of the business cycle, downturns in economic activity led to unemployment and diminished incomes. As such prudent and preventive actions by laid-off workers were difficult.

Also it has been the *custom* that police, fire, water and sewer, roads, bridges, freeways, schooling, garbage collection, and airports are provided by one level of government or another. Custom aside, many of these functions could be provided by private firms on long term contracts to government, or operated outright as private businesses with greater efficiency and at lower cost.

Most Western European nations from Sweden to Italy, from Greece to Great Britain have large public sectors that produce market goods such as electricity, telephone, train and air services. By contrast the US government produces electricity only in the states of Tennessee and Washington but chooses instead to tax, spend, regulate and underwrite as its means of expediting private and public purposes. All of these governmental activities create a vast bureaucracy of public servants with generous salaries, fringe benefits, pensions and other benefits. So while the public in general and specific groups receives benefits, the other winners are the government employees who implement these varied and sundry public programs.

Another variant of the *supplemental* role of government results from what economists call the concept of *public goods and public bads*. One way to illuminate this concept is by contrast to private goods and services in which costs and benefits are equated in market prices, and only then do transactions occur between buyers and sellers. Depending on our incomes and tastes, we buy as much as we wish of food, shelter, clothing, entertainment, etc. We exchange our income claim checks for private goods. How do we obtain claim checks upon our economy? By legal and illegal means. Legally most of us obtain claim checks (money) by working directly, from investment income, and from inheritance. Those not working obtain legal claim checks from governmental programs and private charity. Illegally claim checks flow to individuals and groups from crime of all sorts.

However flowing from these private transactions there may be spillover benefits or costs as the case may be onto third parties. Economists have long labeled these spillovers as "externalities". Since the 1970s without the grace of courses in economics, we have all become aware of various *pollutions* of the air and water as *public bads*.

Yet much economic activity including the making of steel, rubber, chemicals, paints, dyes, leather, and much of agriculture contributes to the production of wastes that in the past have entered the common realm of stream, river, ocean and air as pollution. In short the price of the final consumer good did *not* include the spillovers.

To be sure, recycling is an important method of reducing pollution by industry and by individuals even in the home. Nor were communist and socialist economies exempt from this disregard of spillovers and failure to recycle as the polluted Baltic Sea on the doorstep of the former Soviet Union, Poland and the former East Germany illustrated. Fortunately, the reunification of Germany led to the immediate shutdown of unsafe nuclear and polluting industrial plants in the former eastern portion of the country.

Where the market price cannot capture all of the bad effects, these spillovers constitute a partial public bad. How to solve this market imperfection? Aside from recycling economists have urged taxing these *bad* externalities so that the *two parties to the transaction would primarily bear the costs*. But legislative approaches on the federal and state levels have instead regulated via a cumbersome procedure as one law after another has been added spinning out endless red tape (regulations) to the delight of bureaucrats, but to the detriment of a cleaner environment.

A public service should be distinguished from a public good. The latter may be provided by any collective group be it a trade association or trade union. As to government, whenever it charges a price to consumers for public services, it is a price for admissions to zoos, parks and to buy stamps from the post office.

A public or collective good once enacted by law usually has an *all or nothing* aspect to it. Police and fire protection, and public schooling come under this rubric. Why? While taxpayers enjoy the benefits of these services, they cannot be denied to the newly born, tourists, the homeless and others who pay no taxes. They are free riders for varying amounts of time.

The all or nothing aspect provides a Euclidean lever to proponents to have their pet projects funded. For example, a partial or half completed aircraft carrier is of no value to national defense except as a possible negotiating bargaining chip at disarmament talks. Similarly half completed public buildings are of limited or no value. Hence politicians have long known that "white elephants" can be built at excessive public expense once concrete has been poured beyond a critical point. For example, over-runs on new Congressional office buildings come to mind. Rarely are these domestic or military "white elephants" cancelled.

A more telling illustration of a public or collective good is the *stock* of knowledge. The use by one individual does not diminish the volume of knowledge present. While the stock of knowledge can only be diminished by burning all the libraries and research centers of the world at once (what of human memory?), it still remains true that the *production* of old and new knowledge is a costly enterprise. For example, the publication of the Yellow Pages, almanacs, statistical abstracts, yearbooks and dictionaries involves collection and production costs.

Still another example of a public good occurs when a family watching a TV program does not prevent or deny the tuning in by countless others of the same program. In short, one viewer or an infinite number may see TV programs without denying the next viewer his selection. In other words, the additional or marginal costs of each new viewer are zero. In this vein, the satellite dish is a complication. Some home users object to a user's fee for what they consider to be a "free" item. But the production and transmission costs of public and cable television programs are greater than zero, hence a market price (or donation) is necessary. For commercial television, the price of admission is paid for by the ads.

While some individuals and groups are concerned with global and national public bads, most people are concerned with the micro public bads, which our fellow citizens impose on us daily. As

Thomas Schelling has reminded us, the very *first* piece of litter, the very *first* boom-box on the beach or park or subway, and the very *first* power mower that shatters the Sunday morning calm are all solitary acts that unleash undesirable social behaviors, that is, public bads that are detrimental to the well being of others on the street, bus, park, or in the community.

While a few apologists for the grim graffiti on New York City's subway trains applaud such public disorder, most of those who have had to ride the subway have viewed the acts as vandalism and an affront to their eyes. Also, while the spray paint can and the transistor radio (boom-box) are humble products of our age, they have had in the hands of vandals a *disproportionate effect* on the public environment as instruments and agents of public disorder. Thus government attempts to temper and control the bad spillovers of these social activities much less crime have not been shining successes. Until, that is, the mid 1990s.

Long ago economics textbooks used to consider water and air as "free" goods. Why? Since they were so abundant there was no point in rationing the two items either by pricing or government restrictions. However to many states of the Far West, given its desert like climate, water is relatively scarce, hence water "wars" have erupted over old and current rights to tap this or that river. Drought has compounded the difficulties in California while Mother Nature from time to time has reduced its gifts of rain and snow. Hence water is like any good that depends on a price. Similarly for sewers and treatment plants to keep our rivers, lakes and oceans free from pollution. They are costly. In short there are no free public lunches, anymore, if they ever existed.

The third role of government has been to serve as an instrument to *redistribute income* to a minor or greater degree. If one believes in equality of opportunity then a minor degree of redistribution is desirable to help the less fortunate. If one believes in equality of outcomes regardless of ability, effort and hard work, then a push to equal incomes is desirable. The latter policy goal remains controversial. Some proponents of equality of outcomes have been reluctant to call such policies stepping-stones to a socialist society. Pushing such ideas to their ends would mean displacing the marketplace in favor of central decisions by the federal government much as the Communist Party and bureaucrats of the former Soviet Union determined quantities, quality and the prices of all goods and services as well as the incomes of its people.

The fourth role has involved a modern one since the Great Depression. It has been to use the national budget to *counter the business cycle* by spending, taxing and borrowing policies. But given persistent budgetary deficits by the governments of Western nations including the United States, until 1998. For the most fiscal policy appeared largely ineffective. By default, the only other alternative mechanism was the Federal Reserve (the central bank) to apply monetary policies to counter recessions and inflation.

As we alluded above, a market driven economy of free prices will do much to correct "mistakes" of over and under production. If sales are low and inventories of merchandise are high, the running of "sales" *clears* the market of unsold goods. In short, even goods that are defective, imperfect, or of poor quality can be sold *at a price*. But centrally directed economies lack the immediate feedback that prices and sales figures give. Nor do government central planners have any incentive *to clear markets of unwanted goods*, only to meet annual and five year "paper" quotas of production even if *no one wants the output of goods*.

Thus in the United States our own public sector is in essence a mini-command economy with legislators determining prices, wages, subsidies and other contract terms. Whereas in the private sector whether it be GM or the corner restaurant, if customers stay away and sales decline, the first action is to reduce costs, lay-off workers, seek other economies, re-think the quality of the product or service. And to lower prices. Or face bankruptcy that eventually releases land, labor, capital and materials for new and better uses.

But when public services meet customer resistance or decline in quality, from police, to social workers to education, the first request is to ask for more money, that is, increased taxes (price increase). Thus, typically, there are neither incentives nor the market discipline of bankruptcy to change the outputs of the public sector that are of poor quality.

On the national level, the US Department of Agriculture has blithely given away billions of dollars each year to farmers with the result that consumers pay twice: with higher taxes and higher food prices. While the number of farmers *continuously declines*, the federal handouts to the remaining farmers increase each year sharply.

Also thanks to the tariff, which is a sales tax on over 9,000 foreign goods, millions of American consumers are denied goods that often are of better quality and cheaper in price than domestic equivalents. Thus the tariffs and quotas on imports drive the American standard of living downward. As James Bovard notes in *The Fair Trade Fraud*: "The American tariff code is living proof of a political system's inability *to correct its economic mistakes*" (stress added).

The tariff and quotas of course constitute a national industrial policy rewarding some industries and workers with protection while punishing domestic industries and workers and above all American consumers who are either denied foreign products, or who must pay more for domestic versions. Countless consumers receive nothing from federal protection as often there are no domestic versions of foreign goods, or if they exist they are of shoddy quality. Bovard provides numerous examples.

Thus to speak of free trade and fair trade in the same breath is a contradiction in terms. Free trade is concerned with *open* markets and the flow of labor, products and capital across national borders. By contrast, fair trade and the phrase beloved of politicians, "a level playing field" is of course an invitation to *closed* markets thereby shutting down the flow of goods, capital and labor. *Many* consumers lose while the *few* protected industries win.

If most tariffs reduce the standard of living of Americans, then the late Sam Walton, the organizing genius of Wal-Mart stores, has raised the standard of living of his customers and of other Americans by forcing Wal-Mart's competitors to serve their customers as well or lose them. By offering reduced prices and superior services to his customers, Sam Walton raised the real incomes of his customers. A dollar or two saved at his store was available to be spent elsewhere.

But there is another aspect that distinguishes market and command economies and that is the amount of *slack* to handle additional demand for goods, innovations, and emergencies. As we discovered during World War II, despite the enlistment of 10 million men and women in uniform there was still a vast reserve army of women and retired people to take their places in war plants and elsewhere in the economy.

Secondly, our economy in peacetime rarely operates plants at full capacity. So there is usually slack to meet additional demand for goods. Thirdly, with the aid of the computer, and corporate reorganization including just-in-time inventory control along with better-trained employees, all of these factors contribute to increasing productivity *and* output. This is largely the secret of our high standard of living. And note well, all of this without operating a plant with double and triple shifts which would raise labor and maintenance costs. Still another example of slack involves calling on firms supplying temporary personnel to meet seasonal and other peak load demands.

Even in the home there is slack. As we mentioned, the prudent purchase of insurance is the first line of defense in the case of emergencies; the rainy-day savings account serves as a shock absorber for unforeseen demands; within the home there are spare facilities: couches, sleeping bags, outdoor tent equipment and campers, etc., that permits the temporary housing of relatives, friends, and others in an emergency. Also, despite zoning laws prohibiting its use, "mother-in-law" apartments in homes create additional housing stock. Old and extra-clothing provide another buffer stock. Lastly, the generous donations of surplus food by the American people to food banks and the Salvation Army comes to mind.

In our society, for example, when a child falls into an abandoned well, spontaneous responses take place by many individuals and business firms who lend heavy equipment, as well as the assistance of the first line of community action: the fire and police departments. When a flood, tornado, earthquake or hurricane takes place, the Red Cross, federal disaster teams, the National Guard and other volunteers augment the local units.

Yet when disasters such as earthquakes struck Mexico and Soviet Armenia, there was no slack in these societies and they were unable or unwilling to utilize the good will, the goods and services of foreigners who wished to help. Waiting for the central government in Mexico City and Moscow to issue orders meant that little or nothing was done or accomplished in the critical few days following the disasters.

So far we have outlined the range of governmental functions. But the key question is why tax me? Even if I want the program, tax *the other fellow*! Thus public programs invite bluffing and shows of indifference so that either the price (taxes) is driven down or shifted to someone else say from property owners to so-called "sin" taxes on alcohol and cigarettes. That is, *if* the public program or service is wanted. On the other hand, aside from individual taxes the total weight of taxes compelled can have serious effects on work incentives, the ability to save for a rainy day, and the ability to plan ahead for emergencies by the use of insurance.

For example at what level of taxation, does the burden become onerous and have detrimental social and economic effects? Consider the following range of possibilities:

All Levels of Government Taxation

```
0               25        50          75          100%
—>>>>————>————>————> Gov't Taxes
—<<<<————<————<————< Citizen $$$
100%            75        50          25          0
0               3mos      6mos        9mos        12mos
————>————>————>———!
```

If tax rates are zero, then the citizen keeps all of his income. To the other extreme, if the government taxes all of income, then the citizen keeps none. But if all levels of government take 25% of the national income, that still leaves 75% to be spent and saved by citizens. If the government takes 50%, then only 50% remains for private purposes (in essence working half the year for the government).

At 100% rates, everyone has become a government employee in round-about fashion. Presumably, the "government would pay" for clothing, food, medical insurance, and the rent, etc., much like being in the armed forces. A small spending allowance per family, too? What would happen to the willingness to work? Would black markets surface?

The second major difficulty with democracies and legislative remedies for market imperfections is that by the nature of the process of hearings, debate, deliberations, compromise, and further debate, the nature of legislative problem solving is *backward gazing as in a rear view mirror*. Or to change metaphors, the legislature takes photographs of reality while life goes on like a never-ending motion picture. Hence when legislatures legislate they invariably battle yesterday's social ills like generals and admirals fighting the last war, anew.

Also, politicians at all levels prefer to play Santa Claus than Scrooge to lobbyists and constituents demanding services. Thus there is a built-in bias of upward government spending regardless of merit, fiscal prudence, or priority of needs. Priority is a word that politicians are frightened of since it involves making judgments and saying that this program is more important than that one. In essence saying "no" to some voters. So by sleight of hand, *all* government programs are priority ones! Hence there are *no* priorities!

For twenty years various political pundits have proposed to make the legislative process more rational by suggesting the adoption of various remedies: a) five year sunset laws to all programs, b) Jimmy Carter's zero-based budgeting, c) the Kennedy and Johnson administrations' call for cost/benefit or cost/effectiveness of government programs d) the creation of the Congressional Budgeting Office in 1974 to ride herd on 535 legislators who would each be King or Queen of the domain, and finally, e) the call for term limitations on the tenure of legislators.

Thus in desperation some reformers have proposed three constitutional amendments to rein in a run-away Congress: a balanced budget amendment, another amendment granting the President the budget line-veto and lastly the limitation of terms in office. Since 1974, Congressional staffs have exploded with an implicit mandate to justify their 18,000 jobs and their bosses' tenure by expanding the scope and reach of the federal government. Since 1995, the creep in Congressional staffs has abated.

The third major difficulty is that politicians by definition are always on duty: they face their constituents, the media, the lobbyists, their supporters, and others in a 360° circle. They are in a fishbowl.

Is there no way out of this legislative appetite for more and more taxes, deficits, regulations, rules and more federal and state employees? Possibly if the President and the Governors were to propose an annual fiscal dividend ranging from 3 to 5% for each taxpayer. Much as corporate presidents nurture stockholders by increased sales and profits thereby increasing dividends and stock prices. Thus all government department heads would have to act as entrepreneurs: looking at the "sales" of their services, pruning dead wood, dropping layers of supervision and regulations, introducing new services or enhancing the quality of older ones at a lower cost. This "quality dividend" should permit an annual cash dividend to the taxpayer.

If no fiscal dividend is forthcoming then as Peter Drucker has advocated the only serious alternative is to privatize countless government programs and services.

8 The Hiding Hand

How has the human race tackled the problem of poverty, the perennial state of affairs? Or as Thomas Hobbes defined this grim state of poverty as a life that was solitary, short, nasty and brutish. Two historical concepts give us a clue as to how we overcame the problem of poverty but not the particulars, namely, the Renaissance, with its notion that "man is the measure of all things" and the Industrial Revolution that unleashed economic growth.

In 1776, a Scottish economist by the name of Adam Smith provided the initial set of clues and recommendations in his inquiry as to the causes of the *Wealth of Nations*. Smith essentially urged that the marketplace predicated on private property with its "invisible hand" of flexible market prices would be far superior in channeling human efforts into meeting human satisfactions daily than governmental taxation, regulations, subsidies for favored groups, and confiscations of property on one basis or another.

The "invisible hand" would *only* work if public agencies and private firms did not seek to fix or rig prices to the favor of one group or another but to the detriment of the many. Smith attacked too the policy of mercantilism which held the notion that a nation became prosperous by exporting more than it imported thereby receiving gold and silver to make up for the deficit. To the mercantilist view, a rich country was one that exported real goods while importing ingot bricks of gold and silver that wound up in the basement of the national treasury.

Aside from stressing the superiority of harnessing individual self-interest through the marketplace, Smith also urged two collateral principles of specialization and division of labor as likely to lead to greater production and hence greater consumption of goods and services. If one nation specialized in wine growing and another in cotton growing, both nations could produce *more* of each, and by trading both would enjoy higher standards of living if there were no hindrances such as tariffs, quotas and other devices to stunt trade. In economics textbooks, this principle is known as comparative or relative advantage.

Therefore politicians who speak of a "level playing field" (as we noted in the preceding chapter) seek to nullify the benefits of international specialization and hence trade. Thus when politicians speak again of "fair trade" instead of free trade, they are basically protecting a particular domestic company from competition. But protectionist tariffs, quotas and anti-dumping duties deny American consumers and business firms foreign products and machinery otherwise unavailable within the domestic economy. Or if available at higher prices and of inferior quality. Hence if each nation did not trade at all, world living standards would plunge sharply. Illustrating this truth, the Smoot-Hawley tariff of 1930 passed by Congress and signed by President Hoover signaled a sharp decline in international trade and turned a mild recession in our economy into the Great Depression. All this despite the advice of 1,000 economists who had urged President Hoover to veto the bill as not in the national interest!

After World War Two, economists categorized nations as rich and poor societies including the devastated economies of Germany and Japan. Today, the forthright label of poor nations has been supplanted by countless euphemisms: "less developed nations," "Third World countries," and former Second World "Communist societies" and so on. However in the heady days after the war, before the Cold War was cast in iron curtains, economists were called upon to shed light as to how poor nations might become rich. Some thought, particularly politicians in newly freed colonies in Africa and Asia, that moving from poverty to riches could be done overnight. Today some fifty years later, some of these nations are *poorer* than they were as colonies despite government-to-government grants, subsidized food, and loans, despite private bank, and World Bank loans, and despite private assistance from church groups such as the Quakers. And despite the efforts as well of idealistic Americans in the Peace Corps.

In fact, Great Britain and the United States took two centuries of preliminary preparation in terms of political and social cohesion before economic development moved rapidly. So the idea of a short cut in one generation that leaps from a backward society to a modern one has had to be abandoned. Instead some African nations sought to modernize quickly by adopting the *symbols* of development, a national airline and a steel plant plunked down in the middle of nowhere.

The airline invariably hired foreign pilots and the steel plant shortly began to rust without the necessary infrastructure—the social skeleton of ports, airports, roads, railroads, telephones and power utilities. Also missing were maintenance and spare parts much less a supply of managerial, technical and skilled labor. These physical and human capital items take time to build and develop, are costly and the benefits are delayed. But the leaders of poor countries were in a rush and could not wait. Overnight the national logo was painted on a used airplane. Catapulted into the jet age, Ghana, Uganda and other nations settled for this *detour* from the painful and slow process of modernization.

Others in Africa were lulled by the siren call of Marxism and its chief practitioner the former Soviet Union. African leaders apologized for the lack of literacy, poverty and more by insisting that all power had to be concentrated in a supreme leader working with a single political party to direct all the resources of the nation under the banner of socialism. Tanzania comes to mind. But foreign tourists have discovered in many of these countries that the hotels lack soap or light bulbs in the rooms among other shortcomings. In short, the leaders insisted that freedom was a luxury of rich countries. Despite slogans and rhetoric poverty remained the reality.

However it should be noted that while a nation may be poor, its leaders might accumulate vast wealth by bribery and corruption and drain these ill-gotten efforts into Swiss banks. Ferdinand and Imelda Marcos in the Philippines, the Duvaliers in Haiti, Noriega (before his capture) in Panama, and Mobutu in Zaire among others come to mind easily. The whole or the nation may be a basket case of poverty, but the few live sumptuously and contemptuously off their own people.

Along the way we have discarded the notion that a country is rich because it sits on vast natural resources such as iron, coal, and oil. Japan has virtually none of the three, but is obviously not poor. Similarly the recent rapid development of Taiwan and South Korea, also countries without natural resources has reaffirmed this truth. Oddly enough many African nations in fact have abundant natural resources such as oil in Nigeria, copper in Zaire and basic commodities in other African nations. Whereas the prosperity of Hong Kong and Singapore as city states with no natural resources have confirmed that Adam Smith was on to something of value over two centuries ago.

The collapse of communism has meant that Russia and the other nations of the former Soviet Union face daunting challenges in both establishing democratic institutions and an economy predicated on the rule of law, private property and the laws of supply and demand. If accomplished, the task will take generations.

The *basics of modernization* include a literate population, a reliable and trained work force, individuals and groups willing to take risks in starting businesses that are also alert to world markets. Above all, they must be flexible enough to respond to market price signals. Also the government must provide the first requisite of economic development a stable, honest, and supportive environment for the marketplace. That means private property must be secure, the currency must be inflation free, and the national government budget balanced.

While Western economists in the 1950s visited, observed, and advised the poor nations, what remained of their experiences? One of the economists who advised a number of countries after World War Two was Albert O. Hirschman, a professor of economics, at Harvard, initially and later at Princeton University. If his advice and that of others did not lead to instant prosperity some hard won conclusions did emerge. Looking back over twenty years of experience in tackling the problem of poverty, he enunciated the principle of the hiding hand.

As Hirschman wrote "...the Hiding Hand can accelerate the rate at which men engage successfully in problem solving: they take up problems *they think* they can solve, find them more difficult than expected, but then, being stuck with them, attack willy-nilly the unsuspected difficulties—and sometimes even succeed." (Italics in original.) Thus whether it was a paper pulp plant, a hydroelectric facility, port facilities, or railroad building, it is important that entre-preneurs and planners think a project is feasible. If they were com-pletely aware of what lay in store in terms of disasters and other unintended consequence, no action would be forthcoming.

In our own history think of the laying of the tracks of the Union Pacific railroad, or the construction of the Panama Canal. They are both tales of accomplishment worthy of a second look. Both projects vividly illustrate the hiding hand.

But once the excessive optimism gives way to nasty realities, unforeseen individual resilience, creativity and fresh responses tackle these new sub-sets of problems. Above in "Tools of the Trade" we introduced the concept of bracketing. The Hiding Hand is an example of bracketing where optimism overshoots the target while unexpected reserves of initiative, ideas and new combinations of actions are brought to the surface. As a result the targets are incrementally broached. Central planning by contrast assumes problem-free and friction-free means to achieve goals, at least on paper.

Consider the operation of the hiding hand under the most severe state of affairs: wartime. During World War Two, Allied bombing of Germany was substantial. The bombing killed people, and destroyed plants, yet strangely as Albert Speer, economic czar under Hitler, revealed in his autobiography that thanks to his flair for organizing and reorganizing all the resources at his hand, material and human, he was able, despite the bombings and destruction of war plants, to *increase* war production in due course. But the ground war against Germany, not the bombing, eventually nullified Speer's organizing efforts.

Speaking of military matters, John Kiser has reminded us that the hiding hand has played a vital role in Soviet military weapons development, too. The key problem that Soviet scientists and engineers faced was the shortage of sub-contractors that Boeing, General Dynamics, Martin Marietta, Lockheed, and other principal contractors take for granted in our market economy. The sub-contractors in our society illustrate Adam Smith's principal of division of labor and also the presence of special aptitudes, capacities and know-how. The Soviets had none of these but they, too, had the hiding hand at work. Of course the Soviets had also the KGB, which stole, bribed spies, and bought in the international underworld market all kinds of high tech equipment that were legally prohibited for export by the U.S.

So how did the hiding hand work in the Soviet Union? Their scientists knew they could not match U.S. weapons for complexity, sophistication and costliness. So they opted for simplicity, ruggedness and relatively cheaper weapons. For example, the Kalashnikov rifle, so beloved of terrorists, drug dealers and Mafia the world over, is simple, rugged and cheap to make. The T-34 tank of World War II fame was a modification of an American tank. As Kiser noted, the T-34 design was simplified "for Soviet manufacturing conditions, its mobility, armor protection and firepower improved." As you simplify the design stage, you make it easier for workers to build and assemble the final production with fewer defects. Parenthetically, Kiser notes that "Cheap and simple solutions do not generate much enthusiasm" in the United States. Like a Model T Ford, it has no sex appeal, today. In other words, the Model T is yesterday's dead dream whereas today we welcome complexity.

So the Soviets despite a lemon economy had a military sector that had succeeded, relatively, by adopting a principle which Henry David Thoreau enunciated repeatedly: "simplify, simplify and simplify, again."

Curiously one domestic American company, the Maytag Corporation, has practiced this principle. Its ads have repeatedly pointed to the loneliness of its repairmen. How did the company achieve this desirable state for its customers? Initially, in its clothes washers, the company's engineers eliminated 40% of the parts in the motor and transmission unit. Also the wash basket was produced as a seamless item. Thus steel welds which invite rust and breakdowns were also eliminated. The result was efficiencies in assembly and durability for the customer.

However, Maytag later bought a cluster of minor other brands of home appliances that were inferior in finish, drive train durability and assembly. Clearly the company had its hands full in teaching the newly acquired management and staff people of the new subsidiaries what the Maytag culture of problem solving was all about.

A concluding word about bureaucracies that shun the hiding hand at all costs. The crumbling of the Berlin Wall and implicitly of Marxism does not mean that governmental bureaucracies everywhere have decided to close-up shops and take a holiday. In fact they are more entrenched than ever. Statism, the relentless growth of government, without the clothing of ideology lives on. The so-called European Common Market means that while passports within the market will be obsolete, and goods and services will flow without the impediments of customs, a new super government of bureaucrats located in Brussels has emerged spinning out reams of regulations.

So the benefits of a common market, which permits economies of scale flowing from division of labor, research and development and mass production, will be reduced to the extent that the overhead costs of both new regulations and of bureaucrats receiving handsome salaries, travel and other fringe benefits will serve as deadweight costs. In short, government bureaucrats will be skimming off the cream of economic success much as the Mafia skimmed, at least in the past, business receipts at Las Vegas casinos. In general, when bureaucrats win, the public loses.

After all the French have had central bureaucrats directing the life of the country before Marx, before the Revolution of 1789 and all going back to Louis XIV in the 17th Century. The losers in this dismantling of Marxist ideology have been Western academics, journalists, writers, fellow travelers and other assorted true believers. Their God of St. Marx is dead.

In America, back-door socialism is the preferred device. Rather than abolish private property and the marketplace, both federal and state governments prefer to lay ribbons of red tape on private businesses, non-profit agencies and private universities and colleges. Every business has to pay and collect income or corporate taxes, Social Security and Medicare taxes, unemployment compensation taxes, workers' compensation taxes and property taxes. Homeowners, too, pay their property taxes along with sales taxes and excise taxes on purchases. Then there are regulations and annual reports required of businesses annually on pensions, safety, environmental matters, affirmative action, the hiring of the disabled and more that are costly and a deadweight. Also annual licenses or permission are required from governments on all levels to engage in certain occupations or lines of work.

Then businesses must also contend with trade unions that at times have shown sharp resistance to flexible work rules. When a business sank into bankruptcy, the union practice has been to denounce foreign business firms for not "playing on a level field" by luring American jobs away. Sound familiar?

Nor have local governments at all times sought to promote economic growth, but rather its contraction. Some such as New York City and Berkeley governments have made recruiting a local work force difficult by imposing rent controls. The winners of rent control are tenants who reap a permanent windfall while the losers are the landlords, business community and ultimately the entire community in lost opportunities: as new housing is curtailed or brought to a standstill, unemployment increased, and lower tax receipts from depressed property assessments.

Does the hiding hand have applications to individuals aside from nations and corporations? Indeed it does. If a nation requires the minimal structure of order, literate population, and an infrastructure of transportation and communication, then an individual must be literate, must be increasingly conversant with computers and must have an affinity for problem solving. *Raw labor without any skills whatsoever is very inefficient, inflexible and poorly paid.*

How can poor individuals become prosperous? The wrong way is to look for a shortcut like winning the lottery. Or inheriting wealth. A few do but most people have to either earn a living or become parasitic criminals whether of the white-collar scam variety or the common thug. Both are analogous to believing that in order to be prosperous countries need coal, iron and oil, a *natural* inheritance. On the other hand, the lottery is analogous to believing that Marxism and dictatorship provide a quick easy path to success. The inheritance route presupposes that a nation needs abundant material resources of oil, coal and iron to become wealthy. The third is the way of dictators marching into lands to rape, plunder and steal as Hitler in Poland (1939) and Saddam Hussein in Kuwait (1990) exemplify.

For most people, there are no free lunches. There are no short cuts unless one believes in corruption and the Mafia. Prosaically what individuals need initially is a belief in themselves, or self-confidence, then a set of challenges to be tackled, as their energies are unleashed. Secondly, individuals need to develop the necessary "know-how" of skills and knowledge.

In chapter five we took note of the important role parents play in shaping attitudes, laying down long term plans and goals and proffering the means to achieve them, such as college tuition. Others such as friends, relatives, and teachers may also play supporting roles. Even with support, life has its way of springing surprises, often unwanted. At such times, our hidden abilities surface to meet the daily challenges of life.

Human affairs are for the most part not conducted in an atmosphere of *total information or total ignorance*. The former state is the province of the Deity while lesser mortals seek to avoid the latter or slip into permanent poverty. The *relevant range* is somewhere between these two extreme poles. The hiding hand suggests that there is wide latitude for human action between these two ends. Thus the hiding hand permits some cautious optimism in human affairs tempered by the willingness to avoid quick fixes, political rhetoric and other diversions from the world of work.

Finally the principle of the hiding hand is no miracle cure or "drug" (of take two aspirin and call me in the morning) but rather a cautious optimistic belief in the flowering of human capacities and creativities in a free society. However at times the challenge and difficulties may be so overwhelming that human ingenuity, singly or collectively, cannot salvage a project or product. It is then time to move on to the next challenge of life.

9 Hatfields and McCoys!

Thus far we have been concerned with how individuals, groups and societies go about solving problems. For the most part, the mundane problems of food, shelter, clothing, entertainment and more are solved as we saw through the marketplace as buyers and sellers meet. In turn goods and services are exchanged in varying quantities, qualities and prices.

But when individuals, groups and nations vie for things such as territory, power, wealth, status, security and symbolic goods, we slide often from problem solving to conflict resolution. On a minor scale, the city, county, state and Congressional legislative arenas are places where minor civil wars take place daily. Sometimes legislators actually engage in physical violence; or military forces in a coup d'etat invade legislative buildings; or legislators find their hallowed halls of debate burned down by enemies of democracy. One example is the Reichstag fire in Nazi Germany.

But when the community consensus over what is possible and desirable is breached, then civil war may ensue. Dividing the nation, the issue of slavery led to a dead-end. War followed. Today abortion is an issue too that seemingly knows no compromise.

Then what are the differences between social and economic problems versus conflicts that rend the political fabric? The marketplace permits the necessary problems of feeding, sheltering and clothing a nation to be subdivided into a series of lesser problems handled by numerous suppliers of goods and services. These basic problems are *limited in scope, without emotional baggage* (after all how excited can anyone get over soap, napkins, diapers, etc.?) and are *subjected to individual choice*. And through it all, as Adam Smith understood so well, *competitive markets* in products and labor *lead to social cooperation and stability*.

As such most problems are limited in extent and duration. By contrast, conflicts are open-ended, persistent and regenerative. For one, conflicts by contrast can know no boundary or duration. Like the feuds of the Hatfields and McCoys they may go on forever. For another, they involve a heavy residue of emotions involving hatred, envy, anger, and revenge. The emotional fervor is spent not over mundane matters but over questions of prestige, influence, identity, and power as to who will be top dogs. In these situations and circumstances, the use of violence commences.

Still another dimension of conflicts over time is that the use of violence becomes self-justifying ("they" did it to us, "we" do it to them; "the blood of our brothers must be avenged!"). Headlines daily remind us of numerous tribal and ethnic rivalries that fester over time and are rekindled into bloodletting such as the clashes of Arab/Israeli, Armenians and Azerbaijani, Bosnians and Kosovars against Serbs in the former Yugoslavia.

Closer to home, from Los Angeles to New York City, gang members maim and kill each other over "dissing." Lack of respect shown is an old knee-jerk response among young males as countless Mafia movies illustrate as well.

Furthermore, an individual search for security and order may be non-existent in the face of gang warfare, drug peddling, disease and neighborhood decay. In such a setting despite individual precautions, horrible and tragic events take place. Thus conflicts sharpen identities whether they are of ethnic, religious or neighborhood origins.

Yet not all conflicts lead to violence. Why not? Partly because of countervailing tendencies in all social relations. For example, we have mentioned individual routine as a key element in daily problem solving. When individual inertia is combined with institutional inertia, you have an *initial great barrier* to the chants and shouts of would be advocates of violence.

Secondly, in any complex society, many individuals and groups are vying for mutually contradictory aims, which happily *nullify each other* and mute the siren of screams. Thirdly, to a limited extent, the raising of conflicts creates not only spatial boundaries implicitly, but also *personal identities*. At this point, the contestants may be satisfied with such recognition. And such recognition may lead eventually to legislative legalization as when the labor strikes from the 1880s to the 1930s led to the national Wagner Act permitting collective bargaining. Thus *violent conflicts* between labor and management were turned into normal *problem solving*.

Fourthly, the authorities may choose to nip in the bud any conflict that seriously impinges on society although the 1960s witnessed university officials, politicians, and other authorities acquiescent in the destructive behavior of rioters and demonstrators. One of the dangers of permitting small-scale eruptions is that they escalate into major ones. Parents or teachers may indulge individual temper tantrums, but they may also lead to more frequent outbursts. Group temper tantrums are even more volatile as they lead to looting, raping and arson, in short, a riot.

Lastly, authorities are prone, on the other hand, to do nothing, on the bases of two contradictory premises: 1) ignore the demonstrators or rioters and they will go away, or 2) that "things must get worse before they get better." Both premises draw analogies from medicine in that the best cure at times is benign neglect of the patient. In this case, Mother Nature works presumably its restorative wonders. This inaction has a certain appeal provided it does not lead to the death of the sick person or the destruction of neighborhoods, or of society.

What can we expect from our political leaders? Or are most politicians concerned only with two issues, getting, and staying elected. John F. Kennedy's *Profiles in Courage* revealed how rare that quality is practiced in political life. We mentioned above that politicians are by nature individuals who basically camp out and face all comers in a 360° manner. They cannot hide. They may choose to sympathize with all groups. They may further choose to become demagogues in whom passions are inflamed, and the road to civil war welcomed.

In conclusion, problem solving for many people lacks excitement and is often taken for granted until the electricity goes off, the water stops running and normal life ceases as during a hurricane or earthquake. On the other hand conflicts engender passions that while "entertaining" for the participants have the option of leading to violence. For the most part, problem solving is concerned with shedding light on human affairs, conflicts with bestowing fire and heat. Another way of expressing the difference is to note that problem solving is forward looking while conflict nurturing is backward gazing.

Bibliography
Reading List

The books and articles listed below are meant to be part and parcel of the act of problem solving. As such an introduction to current and past problems serves a spur to further research by utilizing the full array of library reference resources including among others the card catalog, various indexes such as the *Wall Street Journal* and the *New York Times*, the *Reader's Guide to Periodical Literature*, the various publications of the US Government, especially the annual US *Statistical Abstract*. Lastly there are computer on-line services in libraries such as InfoTrac and the search engines of the Internet.

Books

Angell, Marcia. *Science on Trial*. New York: W. W. Norton, 1996.

Bennett, J. T. & DiLorenzo, T. J. *Official Lies: How Washington Misleads* Us. Alexandria, Va.,: Grooom Books, 1992.

Blankenhorn, David. *Fatherless in America*. New York: Basic Books, 1995.

Bovard, James. *The Fair Trade Fraud.* New York: St. Martin's Press, 1991.

Bovard, James. *The Farm Fiasco.* San Francisco: Institute for Contemporary Studies, 1989.

Cox, W. Michael & Alm, Richard. *Myths of Rich and Poor.* New York: Basic Books, 1999.

Crittenden, Danielle. *What Our Mothers Didn't Tell* Us. New York: Simon & Schuster, 1999.

Cronon, William. *Nature's Metropolis: Chicago and the Great West.* New York: W. W. Norton, 1991.

Easterbrook, Gregg. *Moment On the Earth: The Coming Age of Environmental Optimism.* New York: Viking, 1995.

Ferguson, Niall, ed., *Virtual History: Alternatives and Counterfactuals* (London: Papermac, 1997).

Garreau, Joel. *Edge City.* New York: Doubleday, 1991.

Gleick, James, *Chaos: Making a New Science.* New York: Viking Penguin, 1987.

Gross, Martin L. *The Government Racket 2000: All New Washington Waste from A to Z.* New York: Avon Books, 2000.

Landsberger, Henry A. *Hawthorne Revisited.* Ithaca, N.Y.: Cornell University, 1958.

Kelling, George L. & Coles, Catherine M. *Fixing Broken Windows: Restoring Order and Reducing Crime in Our Communities.* New York: Free Press, 1996.

Kramer, Rita. *In Defense of the Family: Raising Children in America Today.* New York: Basic Books, 1983.

Kwitny, Jonathan. *Acceptable Risks*. New York: Poseidon, 1992.

Lovelock, J.E. *Gaia: A New Look at Life on Earth*. New York: Oxford University Press, 1979.

McCullough, David G. *The Path Between the Seas: the Creation of the Panama Canal*. New York: Simon & Schuster, 1977.

McCullough, David G. *The Great [Brooklyn] Bridge*. New York: Simon & Schuster, 1972.

Magnet, Myron. *The Dream and the Nightmare*. New York: William Morrow, 1993.

Michaels, Patrick J. *Sound and Fury: The Science and Politics of Global Warning*. Washington, D.C.: Cato Institute, 1992.

Popenoe, David. *Disturbing the Nest*. NY: Aldine De Gruyter, 1988.

Scott, James C. *Seeing Like a State: How Certain Schemes to Improve the Human Condition Have Failed*, New Haven: Yale University Press, 1998.

Simon, Julian L. *The Ultimate Resource* 2. Princeton: Princeton University Press, 1996.

Sobel, Dava & Andrews, William J. H. *Longitude*. New York: Walker and Co., 1998.

Sowell, Thomas. *Preferential Policies: An International Perspective*. New York: William Morrow, 1990.

Sowell, Thomas. *Markets and Minorities*. New York: Basic Books, 1981.

Stevens, Joseph E. *Hoover Dam: an American Adventure*. Norman: University of Oklahoma Press, 1988.

Sykes, Charles J. *A Nation of Victims: The Decay of the American Character*. New York: St. Martin's Press, 1992.

Thomas, Andrew Petyon. *Crime and the Sacking of America.* Washington, D.C.: Brassey's, 1994.

Tucker, William. *Vigilante: The Backlash Against Crime in America.* New York: Stein & Day, 1985.

Tucker, William. *The Excluded Americans: Homelessness and Housing Policies.* Washington, D.C.: Regnery Gateway, 1990.

Weinberg, Robert A. *One Renegade Cell: How Cancer Begins* (New York: Basic Books, 1998.)

Wildavasky, Aaron. *Searching for Safety.* Transaction Books. New Brunswick: Rutgers University Press, 1988.

Postrel, Virginia. *The Future and Its Enemies: The Growing Conflict Over Creativity, Enterprise, and Progress.* New York: Free Press, 1998.

Articles

[Rather than by author, the articles are topically grouped.]

1. Principle of the Hiding Hand & Problem Solving

Hirschman, Albert O., "The Principle of the Hiding Hand," *The Public Interest*, Number 6, (Winter 1967), 10-23. (In *Longitude*, above, John Harrison solved the problem of how to determine longitude by time keeping.)

Gilder, George, "Zero-Sum Folly, From Kyoto to Kosovo," *Wall Street Journal*, May 6, 1999, p. A26. A positive-sum world is preferable to a zero-sum one.

Gladwell, Malcolm, "Six Degrees of Lois Weisberg," *The New Yorker*, January 11, 1999, pp. 52-63. An illustration of the hiding hand in people "networking" by serendipity.

Kiser, John W., "What US Business Can Learn From Leninism," Wall *Street Journal*, January 3, 1991, p. A10. Kiser reveals how Soviet scientists and engineers to make up for lack of sub-contractors and sophisticated technology applied the hiding hand.

Prud'Homme, Alex, "Off the Urban Rust Heap, a Factory Goes to Work," *New York Times*, January 10, 1999, Section 3, pp. 1, 8. An illustration of the hiding hand in urban revival of decaying neighborhoods.

Selz, Michael & Mehta, Stephanie N. "Business Revitalization In One Missouri Town Has Flood as Its Source," *Wall Street Journal*, September 11, 1996, pp. A1, A10. The hiding hand in practice using a flood as an opportunity rather than defeat.

2.   Accidents and Disasters as Catalysts

Anon., "Escape: Because Accidents Happen," NOVA, *PBS-TV*, February 16, & 17, 1999. This four-part program examines the result of accidents in fire, car and plane crashes and ship-sinkings that lead eventually to solutions.

Mathews, Anna Wilde, "Six Seconds, 2 Dead: A Police Van Crash Exposes a Bombshell," *Wall Street Journal,* November 1, 1999, pp. A1, A38. Driver error or mechanical defect? Sleuth investigates cause and discovers a surprise.

Pascall, Glenn, "Major National Disasters Require Balanced Reaction from Leaders," *Seattle Times*, April 23, 1989, p.E7 on media reaction to various accidents of the last twenty years including Three Mile Island, Apollo 1967 accident, the Santa Barbara and Valdez oil spills.

Fialka, John J. "Dust Storm: Fear of a Different Sort of Infiltrator Paralyzes U.S. Nuclear Project," *Wall Street Journal,* December 20, 1999, pp. A1, A17. At Livermore, CA, a new nuclear ignition facility was late and over budget. Why?

Anon., "Meltdown at Three Mile Island," *The American Experience*, *PBS-TV*, February 22, 1999.

Carley, William M., "In a Big Plane Crash, Cause Probably Isn't Everybody's Guess," *Wall Street Journal*, March 29, 1988, pp. 1,21. The article offers good examples of *jumping to conclusion* in the media's handling of airplane crashes.

Carley, William M. "United 747's Near Miss Sparks a Widespread Review of Pilot Skills," *Wall Street Journal*, March 19, 1999, pp. A1, A8.

Glassner, Barry, "Fear of Flying," *Wall Street Journal*, November 2, 1999, p. A26. After each plane crash, the media's tendency to hype fears of flying by citing slanted statistics and coincidences.

Pasztor, Andy & Mathews, Anna Wilde, "Why More Plane-Crash Probes End in Doubt," *Wall Street Journal*, March 22, 1999, pp. B1, B4.

Poole, Robert H., "For Safer Skies, Privatize," *Wall Street Journal*, February 11, 1991, p. A10. The author observes that "Obsolete equipment, inadequate staffing at key choke-points, and predictably poor morale plague the air traffic control system." The solution is to remove the federal government from this inferior system.

3.   Medical Problems

Naik, Gautam, "In Sunlight and Cells, Science Seeks Answers to High-Tech Puzzles," *Wall Street Journal*, January 26, 1996, pp. A1, A5. Research labs engaged in searches of new problem solving techniques from evolution to T-cells. (See above, Robert Weisberg's, *One Renegade Cell*.)

Langreth, Robert & Moore, Stephen, "Gene Therapy, Touted as a Breakthrough, Bogs Down in Details," *Wall Street Journal*, October 27, 1999, pp. A1, A6. No easy fix for diseases.

Weiss, Rick, "Study: 98,000 Deaths Each Year Are Linked to Medical Mistakes," *Seattle Times*, November 30, 1999, pp. A1, A24.

The headline neglected the range of mistakes from 44,000 to 98,000. Physicians, pharmacists and other health care professionals make the medical mistakes.

Stolberg, Sheryl Gay, "Do No Harm: Breaking Down Medicine's Culture of Silence," *New York Times,* December 5, 1999, Section 4, pp. 1, 18. The writer also uses the 98,000 figure in the main article and in a small insert on p. 18, "Calculating Costly Mistakes," the writer mentioned the range from 44,000 to 98,000 based on different studies.

Jenkins Jr., Holman W. "Let GE Fix the 'Medical Errors' Problem," *Wall Street Journal,* December 15, 1999, p. A23. The federal government is the principal source of medical mistakes via Medicare rigging of prices and regulations.

Weinstein, Michael M. "Checking Medicine's Vital Signs," *New* report cards on health plans to reduce the horrendous mistakes made in hospitals by doctors and nurses.

Zuger, Abigail, "The Hours That Make A Student an M.D.," *New York Times,* November 21, 1999, Section 4, p. 16. The mistakes that medical interns make because of lack of experience and sleep, and the mistakes that occur if when sleep increases.

Talbot, Margaret, "The Placebo Prescription," *New York Times Magazine*, January 9, 2000, pp. 34-39, 44, 58-60. A survey of the medical literature on the uses of placebos by researchers in medical experiments with surprising results. [It may be that the positive effect of placebos may be a variant of the "Hawthorne effect." See Landsberger above.]

4.   Ideas and Experts Redefining Problems

Tierney, John, "Betting the Planet," *New York Times Magazine*, December 2, 1990, pp. 52,53ff. The author relates that doomsayer, Paul Ehrlich lost a ten year bet to Julian Simon that a basket of commodities would be *higher* in price reflecting their *declining* supply, but prices were in fact *lower* as world supplies *increased*.

Lewis, Peter H., "Harnessing the Power of Suggestion,"

New York Times, June 4, 1989,p. 16, Business Section on IdeaFisher, a software program of 675,000 words, a data base of ideas and associations.

Cohen, Laurie P., "Firms Faulted for 'Independent' Inquiries," *Wall Street Journal*, June 14, 1989, p. Bl on the use of outside "experts" to render so-called *impartial* advice to corporations.

Hershey, Robert D., "Capitol Hill's High-Tech Tutor," *New York Times*, July 16, 1989, Sect.3, pp. 1, 12. A report on Congress' Office of Technology Assessment that provides expert analysis and policy options.

White, Gregory L. "GM Takes Advice from Disease Sleuths to Debug Cars," *Wall Street Journal,* April 8, 1999, pp. B1, B4. To reduce defective cars, GM turned to the problem solving techniques of the Center for Disease Controls.

Glaberson, William, "Coping in the Age of 'NIMBY'," *New York Times*, June 19, 1988, Section 3, pp. 1, 25. A summary of various protests and illustration of the Not-in-My-Backyard syndrome.

Kristol, Irving, "Conflicts That Can't Be Resolved," *Wall Street Journal,* September 6, 1997, p. A12. A distinction between therapeutic conflict resolution and mediation.

Drucker, Peter F., "Sell the Mailroom," *Wall Street Journal*, July 25,1989, p. A16. Drucker argues that the key way to improve productivity in government and non-profit agencies is to spin-out many in-house activities such as clerical, maintenance and support work to private contractors.

Payne, James L., "Limiting Government by Limiting Congressional Terms," *The Public Interest*, No. 103 (Spring 1991), 106-117. A prescription for improving the federal government by insuring turnover by set terms of office.

Ricks, Thomas E. "Lessons Learned: Army Devises System to Decide What Does, And Does Not Work," *Wall Street Journal*, May 23, 1997, pp. A1, A10. To avoid fighting tomorrow the last war again and again, the US Army has, with the aid of information technologies, "invented the lessons learned" process.

Stricharchuk, Gregory, "Computer Records Become Powerful Tool for Investigative Reporters and Editors," *Wall Street Journal*, February 3, 1988, p.25. Instead of legwork, reporters can tap into databases to sleuth about.

Nasar, Sylvia, "Women's Progress Stalled? Just Not So: Popular Wisdom Aside, Women Were Big Winners in the 80's, New Data Show, and Gains Should Keep Coming," *New York Times*, October 18, 1992, pp. 1, 10, Section 3. A comprehensive essay citing the work of three economists who challenge the current stereotype that women are falling behind men in remuneration. Also, the three economists are women.

Haywood, Gar Anthony, "They Were Wrong, but I'm Glad They Asked," *Seattle Times*, January 24, 1988, pp. K1, K2 is a classic case of *jumping to conclusion* by a neighbor who heard children screaming and called the police. The police came, saw, and left. Haywood concluded that "with time I came to understand that all too often the truths seen by the naked eye turns out to be lies. Smiles hide demons, and warmth masks madness. External appearances and perfectly rational explanations cannot always be trusted. Clearly, then, the overzealous neighbor who had blown the whistle had acted on the only concrete evidence that she had: the semi-regular cries of a child." This particular child was a screamer for all occasions.

5. What If Scenarios

Boynton, Robert S. "Thinking the Unthinkable," *The New Yorker*, April 12, 1999, pp. 43-46, 48-50. A profile of the historian, Niall Ferguson and "what if" scenarios in history. See Niall Ferguson, *Virtual History*, above.

Rifkin, Glenn, "'What If...' Software For Manufacturers," *New York Times*, October 18, 1992, p. 9, Section 3. Reducing errors and mistakes in business by playing "what if" scenarios.

6. Occam's Razor and Clustering

Anon., "Occam's Disposable Razor: Is Seeing Believing?" *The Economist*, October 5, 1996, pp. 81-82. "Occam here, Occam there, Occam, Occam everywhere—like the barber of Seville, the barber of philosophy has been hoisted by his own popularity." The article explores the principle of parsimony and its history.

Safire, William, "Ockham's Razor Close Shave," *New York Times Magazine,* January 31, 1999, p. 14. Safire explores the principle, its variant spelling and the linking of Occam with the razor metaphor.

Stewart, Ian, "Puzzling Through the Problems," *London Times*, April 6, 1989, p. 31. "But what does it mean to say that a problem is 'hard' or 'easy'?"

Kolata, Gina, "Probing Disease Clusters: Easier to Spot Than Prove," *New York Times,* January 31, 1999, Section 4, p. 6

Anon., "The Complications of (Business) Clustering," *The Economist,* January 2, 1999, pp. 53-54.

Gomesk, Lee & Weber, Thomas E. "Hackers' Weapon Exploits Internet's Open Nature," *Wall Street Journal,* February 10, 2000, pp. B1, B6. Hackers use of short messages in volume that have large effects in shutting down Internet portals.

7. Junk Science: How Not to Solve Problems

Van Natta Jr., Don, "Polling's 'Dirty Little Secret': No Response," *New York Times*, November 21, 1999, Section 4, pp. 1, 16. How accurate are polls when the "no response" rate reaches 80 per cent and is rarely revealed?

Whelan, Elizabeth M., "Apple Dangers Are Just So Much Applesauce," *Wall Street Journal*, March 14, 1989, p. A20. The article reviews the Alar pesticide scare on apples.

Editorial, "How a PR Firm Executed the Alar Scare," *Wall Street Journal*, October 3, 1989, p. A22, from a memo by Fenton Communications detailing its techniques.

Sirkin, Gerald, "The Green Lobby's Dirty Tricks," *Wall Street Journal*, January 2, 1991, p. A6 reveals how one environmental group sought to suppress a study of pesticide regulation in California.

Naj, Amal K., "Not the Cleanest Way to Clear the Air," *Wall Street Journal*, June 19, 1989, p. A10, a critical look at legislative attempts to mandate one approach to the detriment of new technologies.

8. Clean Air & Global Warming:Problem Solving or Politics?

Robinson, Arthur B & Robinson, Noah E. "Global Warming is 300-Year-Old News," *Wall Street Journal*, January 18, 2000, p. A26. See their chart on "Climate in Perspective" from 1000BC to 1998.

Shabecoff, Philip, "In Search of a Better Law to Clear the Air," *New York Times*, May 14, 1989, p.5, Section 4, a summary of the imperfections of the current law.

Pascal Zachary, G., "A Scientist Tracks the World's Fires," *Wall Street Journal*, February 8, 1999, pp. B1, B4. Should forest fires be allowed to burn or combated?

Melloan, George, "Waste Disposal and the 'Environmental Evangelists'," *Wall Street Journal*, July 26, 1988, p. 27. An examination of three *types* of "environmental evangelists": a) true believers, b) failed would-be scientists and c) opportunists and sometime extortionists.

9.   Recycling: Therapy or Problem Solving?

Bailey, Jeff, "Curb Recycling Has Only a Little Effect, A New Study Finds," *Wall Street Journal*, October 4, 1994, pp. A2, A16.

Bailey, Jeff, "Curbside Recycling Comforts the Soul, But Benefits Are Scant," *Wall Street Journal*, January 19, 1995, pp. A1, A8.

Bailey, Jeff, "[Recycling] Marketers Make Extravagant Promises, Then Begin to Regret Them," *Wall Street Journal*, January 19, 1995, p. A8.

Scarlett, Lynn, "Make Your Environment Dirtier—Recycle," *Wall Street Journal*, January 14, 1991, p. A12 notes that recycling proponents have ignored the total cost of one item over another. For example banning the McDonald hamburger polystyrene holder in favor of paper meant higher energy, air and water pollution.

Tierney, John, "Recycling is Garbage," *New York Times Magazine*, June 30, 1996, pp. 24-29, 44, 48, 51, 53. A critical look at the principle and practice of recycling.

Passell, Peter, "Cutting Waste Can Be a Waste," *New York Times*, Section 4, September 21, 1997, pp. 1, 5. Cites economists who cite the trade-offs spent separating garbage, or not eating every scrap of food versus time and income. Or donating one's time rather than simply sending a check!

Warren, Susan, "Recycler's Nightmare: Beer in Plastic," *Wall Street Journal*, November 16, 1999, pp. B1, B4. An oversupply of plastics exists without putting beer in plastic.

10. Environmental Extortion?

Machalaba, Daniel, "As Old Pallets Pile Up, Critics Hammer Them AS a New Eco-Menace," *Wall Street Journal*, April 1, 1998, p. A1. There may be 1.5 billion pallets in the US, made out of hardwoods and piling up since many garbage dumps refuse to accept them. While biodegradable, they fill up space quickly. So they pile up serving as hideaways for rats, raccoons, etc.

Dietrich, Bill, "Watchdogs of the Environment or Extortionists?" *Seattle Times*, December 27, 1988, pp. A1,A4.
Two local attorneys filed environmental appeals on land development then demanded cash payments to drop their appeals.

Greve, Michael S., "Congress's Environmental Buccaneers,"
Wall Street Journal, September 18, 1989, p. A18. Greve notes that under the federal Clean Water Act, most civil suits are "…mass produced by highly professional advocacy groups. Five environmental groups account for more than half of all such actions."

Bovard, James, "Some Waste Cleanup Rules are a Waste of Resources," *Wall Street Journal*, February 15, 1989, p. A16. An examination of some rules that are overly costly or boomerang from their intended effects.

Wartzman, Rick, "A Foe of Fiberglass Tells All Who Listen It's Dangerous Stuff," *Wall Street Journal*, February 26, 1988, pp. 1,6. As to hypotheses, a hypothesis may be new and economical because it has no supporting evidence as the hypothesis that fiberglass is as deadly as asbestos by analogy. The proponent of this view in the above article is a layman and businessman offering a *rival home insulation.* Also for a challenge to the current hypothesis on the *cause* of AIDS, see Katie Leishman, "The AIDS Debate That Isn't," *Wall Street Journal*, February 26, 1988, p. 14. The challenge to orthodoxy in this case comes from a professor of virology.

11. Pollution: Simple or Complex Problems?

Mazmanian, Daniel & Morell, David, "The Elusive Pursuit of Toxics Management," *The Public Interest*, No.90 (Winter 1988), 81-98. Despite many laws, the management of dangerous wastes has proved elusive, as this lengthy review makes clear.

Schmidt, William E., "In the Great Lakes, Some Pollution Defies Cleanup," *New York Times*, July 2, 1989, p.5, Sect.4.
While the surface waters have been improved, the toxics such as the PCBs remain in the sediment of the lakes.

Editorial, "Warming up to the Facts," *Wall Street Journal*, January 11, 1991, p. A10. A British TV producer was unable to sell his documentary, "The Greenhouse Conspiracy," to the PBS-TV network because in their judgment the program was "too one sided."

Miniter, Richard, "PBS: Is the 'Green' Network a Bit Shady?"
Seattle Post-Intelligencer, February 17, 1991, p. D1. Miniter also reviews the contents of "The Greenhouse Conspiracy" and the failure of PBS-TV to air the program.

Bovard, James, "Lester [Brown], the Sky Hasn't Fallen," *Wall Street Journal*, June 26, 1989, p. A10 is an examination of Lester Brown, a prominent Doomsday expert, of the Worldwatch Institute, whose various predictions have *not* materialized.

12. Doomsday Revisited: Diversion or Problem Solving?

Pascall, Glenn, "What Drives the Doomsday Enthusiasts?" *Seattle Times*, March 13, 1988, p. B1. Pascall raises a key question: "Why should anyone's spirits fall upon being told by a supposed expert that, after all, calamity may not occur?" Because "...there is appeal for many in the idea that the world will end."

Bonner, Raymond, "Crying Wolf Over Elephants," *New York Times Magazine*, February 7, 1993, pp. 16-19ff. An expose of a hoax that elephants were in danger of extinction because of their ivory tusks by predators.

Hite, Arnold, "Chicken Little Was Wrong About Oil, Too," *Wall Street Journal*, February 2, 1988, p. 22. Hite takes issue with a full page ad that appeared in January 1976 claiming that within 12 years, the US would run out of proven oil reserves—1988 had arrived and passed with oil flowing at lower prices!

Wald, Matthew L., "An Energy Glut in the Ground Imperils Ecological Hopes," *New York Times*, October 15, 1989, p.5, Section 4, indicates that instead of falling, fossil fuels reserves are *rising*.

Royte, Elizabeth, "Attack of the Microbiologists," *New York Times Magazine*, January 14, 1996, pp. 21-23. An article about Lynn Margulis, co-founder of the Gaia Hypothesis.

Wade, Nicholas, "Method and Madness," *New York Times Magazine*, August 14, 1994, p. 18. A brief discussion of the Gaia Hypothesis and the anthrophic cosmological principle.

Schneider, Keith, "New View Calls Environmental Policy Misguided," *New York Times*, March 21, 1993, pp. 1, 16, National Edition. Schneider observes "that much of America's environmental program has gone seriously awry." At great cost to the taxpayer, with little or no benefit, but with countless bureaucratic jobs created.

13. Graffiti & Broken Windows

Butterfield, Fox, "Graffiti Seems to Be Fading from New York Walls," *New York Times*, May 6, 1988, (national edition), p.12. Butterfield does not consider that graffiti may decline because like epidemics it may fade after time, nor has he considered the policy of public officials in tolerating for decades this outburst of vandalism. [Apropos of government and police officials in tolerating the initial "broken window" as it led to social disorder, so graffiti was tolerated as it led to more and more graffiti. See Kelling, above.]

Kirkpatrick, David D. "American Graffiti: These Tourists Visit and Vandalize," *Wall Street Journal*, August 22, 1996, pp. B1, B7. European tourists for fun and delight have been exporting graffiti especially on New York City trains and walls. These are not ghetto poor but older and middle class tourists from Berlin and elsewhere. Prolonged adolescence?

14.   U.S. Farm Programs: Problem Solving or Politics?

Bovard, James,"Jubilee Time at Farmers Home Administration," **Wall** *Street Journal*, April 26, 1988, p. 30, where Bovard notes "Farm credit handouts are a classic case of ill-conceived humanitarianism. The more the government helps each individual farmer plant, the less all other farmers will receive for their harvest. Every time congressmen say they are helping a farmer, they are subsidizing all other farmers' competition."

Bovard, James, "The Government's Fat Cotton Cushion," *Wall Street Journal*, December 14, 1988, p. A14. Bovard notes, "The federal government justifies paying cotton growers a bonanza as a way to boost exports—but another cotton welfare program is effectively paying farmers not to export."

McInnis, Doug, "Higher Grazing Fees Have Ranchers Running Scared," *New York Times*, September 12, 1993, Section 3, p. 5. Normally, governments charge less than market prices for public land and water usage, but in this case higher fees may not have the intended environmental effect.

15. Truck Safety and Roads

Elsner, David M., "Highway Damage by Big Trucks Worries Various Agencies, and Crackdowns Loom," *Wall Street Journal*, April 6, 1978, p. 40. While the damage grows daily, the crackdowns have not occurred, nor the idea by the US Transportation Department in 1978 to restrict big trucks to a limited number of interstate freeways: "freight corridors."

Poole, Jr., Robert W., "The High Road to Better Highways," *Wall Street Journal*, June 28, 1989, p. A16 is an examination of various states that have permitted private toll roads in the United States.

Yoo, John, "As Highways Decay, Their State Becomes Drag on the Economy," *Wall Street Journal*, August 30, 1989, pp. A1, A8. While the interstate freeway system decays, the federal highway trust fund "boasts an unspent cash balance of more than $14.5 billion."

Whitely, Peyton, "Road Math: Big Trucks Destroying Highways," *Seattle Times*, February 20, 1991, p. D1. Whitely reveals that a single ten-ton truck does more damage to the pavement than 10,000 Toyotas.

16. Unlicensed Drivers and Highway Accidents

Crain, W. Mark, "Spinning Wheels on Old Safety Checks," *Wall Street Journal*, September 25, 1984, p. 28. Annual auto inspections appear to have virtually no effects on reducing road accidents.

Whitely, Peyton, "Unlicensed—and on the Road: We all Pay the Price When Thousands Drive Who Shouldn't," *Seattle Times*, June 30, 1989, pp. A1, A8. Whitely reports that "Between 10 and 20 percent of Washington's (State) drivers may be on the streets without valid driver's licenses" and without auto insurance. [The *problem* is not confined to the state of Washington.]

Karr, Albert R., "Driver Error, the Cause of Most Auto Mishaps, Defies Easy Solution," *Wall Street Journal,* May 4, 1982, pp. 1, 20.

Wong, Jan, "Despite Recent Laws, Many Motorists Are Still Casual About Wearing Seat Belts," *Wall Street Journal*, March 7,1986, p.21. Why are drivers unwilling to buckle-up?

Darlin, Damon, "Does 55-MPH Speed Limit Save Lives? More Drivers are Doubtful," *Wall Street Journal*, April 28, 1986, p. 25. Substantial evidence questions the assumption that higher speeds lead to a greater number of accidents.

Peters, Eric, "Highways Are Safe at Any Speed," *Wall Street Journal,* November 24, 1998, p. A22. Predictions were made that lifting the 55mph speed limit would increase auto deaths, the evidence is in but little publicized.

17. Cultural Tics or Disorder?

Chapman, Stephen, "F-Word March," *The American Spectator*, September 1995, pp. 58-59. [Like "broken windows" and graffiti, the toleration of profanity has contributed to social unease and disorder. Again, see Kelling, above.]

Gabler, Neal, "Talking Trash: Why America Loves It," *Seattle Times*, June 11, 1995, p. B7. Because it is easy and apparently costless in daily affairs.

Lopate, Phillip, "It's Not Heroes Who Have Bad Grammar; It's Films," *New York Times*, Section 2, June 18, 1995, pp. 13,28.

Stossel, John, "Foul Mouthed Children," *20/20* ABC-TV, July 12, 1996.

18. Free Trade, Fair Trade & the Media: Connections?

The World Trade Organization [WTO] met in Seattle, November 29 through December 3, 1999. First note the following criteria for assessing media coverage and then read the following citations.

First, did the press and TV news seek to provide a *context* for the daily events? For example:

1). Did reporters seek answers to basic questions? Of the protest-ers: Who were they? Where did they come from? Who paid their fare to Seattle? What group(s) were they members of? Were these people unemployed? Since, judging from photos and TV coverage, a number of the protesters were young of high school or college age, who recruited them?

2). Did any of the press or TV reporters seek to compile each day a directory of all the groups (with their phone numbers listed and addresses) taking part in the "protests"?

3). As to the notion that the First Amendment permits some peo-ple to prevent other people from entering a public building, or a mob of protesters chaining themselves to the doors of the Westin Hotel in Seattle to achieve the same result, did the press and TV news provide some legal background on these actions? When and where does freedom of assembly for some mean that other Americans have to give up their rights to freely move about? Has the US Supreme Court blessed this behavior and when? As for the local newspaper, did the *Seattle Times* use or call upon the faculty at the University of Washington law school? Did the national newspapers simi-larly call upon legal experts elsewhere for information?

4). Did the press and TV news seek to explain what free trade is all about? Rather than an abstruse depiction of relative and absolute advantage, did they present a catalog in table form of our exports on one side and our imports on the other. This information was fundamental. What is the difference between free trade and fair trade?

5). Did President Clinton demagogue the issue so thoroughly that the WTO in its future negotiations would have to come up with a supposedly, "human face"? The "protesters" objected to what the WTO had done in the past as imperialism and then in the same breath insisted on new labor and environmental rules being foisted on the poorest nations! Was this trade policy akin to junk science, global warning and anti-GMO sweeping Europe? In Seattle, did we witness the new idealism or old-age Luddites and "Know-nothings" of the new millennium?

Nielsen, Susan, "WTO: 50,000 Rabbits and Not a Fact in Sight," *Seattle Times,* November 11, 1999, p. B6. SN outlined some bare facts as to what the WTO can and cannot do, that it is not evil, but "reflects the best and worst of its participant countries..." Destroy the environment? "Not true." She denounces the Roosevelt High School newspaper's editorial as silly when it asserts that the WTO shreds the US Constitution. She sharply criticized the Luddites and know-nothings along with the AFL-CIO, which is in the job protection stance also known as "fair trade".

Anderson, C. Leigh, "WTO Can Move Debate on Trade, Environment to Middle Ground," *Seattle Post-Intelligencer,* November 21, 1999, pp. F1, F3. She is an associate professor in the school of public affairs at the UW. Generally this is a carefully analyzed article on the benefits of free trade. She stresses that free trade is beneficial especially for poorer countries. By raising their incomes it permits poorer nations the opportunity to tackle environmental and social improvements. The one key omission in the article is the role of labor in protecting jobs; and the omission of the principle of comparative advantage, both relative and absolute.

Pemberton-Butler, Lisa, "WTO Issues Unite Students: Teachers Stir Up Interest in Upcoming Trade Talks," *Seattle Times,* November 22, 1999, pp. B1, B2. A Renton High School teacher invited his students to take an interest in the WTO conference in Seattle, and then invited the "protesters" to visit his classroom and spread their point of view, to wit, that free trade thrives on sweatshop conditions overseas. The protesters urged students to be truant on November 30th and protest! The article also noted that student protestors from the UW and Seattle high school would participate! The Renton HS teacher, Dutch Day, said he wanted a different viewpoint to counter-act the media's pro WTO stance. Hence there were no speakers for free trade.

Robin, Joshua, "Keeping the Peace Among [WTO] Protesters," *Seattle Times,* November 22, 1999, pp. B1, B2. Students and AFL-CIO are training peace-monitors and marshals to keep the demonstrations orderly.

Postman, David et. al, "Confusion Grips WTO Warm-Up," *Seattle Times,* November 29, 1999, pp. A1, A14.

Postman, David, "Right Meets Left in Protest, But for Different Reasons," *Seattle Times,* November 29, 1999, p. A12.

Dunphy, Stephen, "Unions Press WTO for Labor Rights," *Seattle Times,* November 29, 1999, p. A13.

Postman, David et. al, "Tear Gas in Streets of Seattle," *Seattle Times,* November 30, 1999, pp. A1, A21

Dunphy, Stephen, "[Ministers] Numbers Low for Besieged WTO Opening," *Seattle Times,* November 30, 1999, pp. A1, A22.

Carter, Mike, "KOMO-TV Announces It Won't Cover 'Irresponsible or Illegal' Activities," *Seattle Times,* November 30, 1999, p. A23.

But the KOMO news director's statement that the station was "taking a stand on not giving some protest groups the publicity they want." This drew a retort from Ben Bagdikian, retired dean of journalism at the U of California Berkeley that the disruptive and illegal protests were "all the more worthy of coverage" both as a public service and to give a voice to the disenfranchised in America!

Cooper, Helene, "Some Hazy, Some Erudite and All Angry: Diversity of WTO Protests Makes Them Hard to Dismiss," *Wall Street Journal,* November 30, 1999, pp. A2, A12.

Melloan, George, "Welcome to the Seattle World's Fair, Circa 1999," *Wall Street Journal,* November 30, 1999, p. A27. "The transition to a world in which 'globalization' makes some jobs less secure, even while it is making the overall economy wealthier, will be more traumatic in Europe than in the U.S., simply because there are more unionized workers enjoying state protections in Europe."
"In Seattle, the demonstrators will demand that the clock be turned back to a simpler age. But that is not going to happen. The folks who can't stand prosperity will ultimately have to yield to those who employ their talents and energies to creating it. It has always been that way."

Broom, Jack et. al, "Protesters Banned, Arrested," *Seattle Times,* December 1, 1999, pp. A1, A12.

Postman, David & Carter, Mike, "Police Switch to New Strategy," *Seattle Times,* December 1, 1999, pp. A1, A14.

Postman, David, "Black-Clad Anarchists Target Cars, Windows and Reject Other's Pleas of 'No Violence'," *Seattle Times,* December 1, 1999, p. A12.

Mcfadden, Kay, "[Local] TV Showed It Made a Difference," *Seattle Times,* December 1, 1999, p. A16. KM lauded KING-TV for its length of coverage and "strength in explanatory reporting and [that] provided a steady stream of context throughout the mayhem."

Cooper, Helene, "Waves of Protest Disrupt WTO Meeting," *Wall Street Journal,* December 1, 1999, pp. A2, A12.

Fukuyama, Francis, "The Left Should Love Globalization," *Wall Street Journal,* December 1, 1999, p. A26. "For the left, American imperialism has evolved into a new enemy, whose name is *globalization.*" (Italics in original.) FF alludes to the fact that foreign workers allegedly working in sweatshop conditions have no alternatives if these jobs are shut down. [In fact many will drift back into grinding poverty and prostitution.] FF believes that the WTO in time will address labor and environmental concerns while governments provide retraining and other subsidies to those laid off.

Nielsen, Susan, "Meaning of [WTO] Protests Blurs in Photo-Op of Century," *Seattle Times,* December 2, 1999, p. B4. She notes that video camcorders and camera were everywhere including the media. "What made the protests real? Mere experience seemed insufficient. Realness now requires the accumulation of proof." Become the media! "That's the positive spin. On the flip side, it's hard for a crowd not to wallow in self-awareness when it reflexively views itself through the lens of a TV camera."

Nelson, Robert T. et. al, "Shoppers Barred in Retail Core," *Seattle Times,* December 2, 1999, pp. A1, A24.

Beason, Tyrone, "WTO Asked to Enforce Child Labor Ban," *Seattle Times,* December 2, 1999, p. A26. Several labor groups called on the WTO to ban child labor and insisted they were not asking for much except a minimum wage in all countries, the right of workers to bargain collectively and safe workplaces.

Harrington, Patrick, "Steelworkers Rally Against WTO, 'Dumping'," *Seattle Times,* December 2, 1999, p. A23. The steelworkers protested against cheap imports from Asia and the admission of China to the WTO.

Matthews, Robert Guy, "U.S. Steel Industry Itself Gets Billions in Public Subsidies, Study Concludes," *Wall Street Journal,* November 29, 1999, p. B16. A study by the American Institute for International Steel reveals heavy federal and state subsidies for U.S. steel makers. The domestic steel companies challenge the study and insist that foreign steel companies receive massive domestic subsidies.

Cooper, Helene, "Poorer Countries Are Demonstrators' Strongest Critics," *Wall Street Journal,* December 2, 1999, pp. A2, A8. What the protestors and organized labor wanted was the opposite of what poorer countries sought.

Editorial, "While the WTO Burns," *Wall Street Journal,* December 2, 1999, p. A22.

Deusterberg, Thomas J. "Free Trade Can Progress Without WTO," *Wall Street Journal,* December 2, 1999, p. A22. Free trade can be achieved from the bottom up through regional accords.

Seib, Gerald F. et. al, "Protests: Face of Future or Just a Blast From the Past?" *Wall Street Journal,* December 2, 1999, p. A8.

Zimmerman, Rachel, "[Seattle] Police Stumble Despite Months of Preparation," *Wall Street Journal,* December 2, 1999, p. A8.

Davis, Bob & Cooper, Helene, "U.S. Worries About Future Trade Talks," *Wall Street Journal,* December 3, 1999, pp. A2, A8.

Postman, David et. al, "Peace Settles Over Downtown," *Seattle Times,* December 3, 1999, pp. A1, A26.

Brunner, Jim & Broom, Jack, "Anarchists: They Play by Different Rules," *Seattle Times,* December 3, 1999, p. A25.

Associated Press, "Anarchists' Guru Says He's Proud," *Seattle Times,* December 3, 1999, p. A25.

Miletich, Steve, "Police Weary After a Long Week," *Seattle Times,* December 3, 1999, p. A22. A photo accompanied this story showing two parents dressed in mock police gear with their nine year old daughter standing between them holding a placard "Citizens Against Police Agression"(sic).

Ith, Ian & Burkett, Janet, "Rally Protests Police Actions," *Seattle Times,* December 3, 1999, p. A22. The police on the night of December 1, directed protestors away from downtown to the Capitol Hill neighborhood and used tear gas and stun grenades to disperse crowds with the result that people in the neighborhood received the spill over of the noise and gas.

McFadden, Kay "KIRO-TV Keeps Eye on Police," *Seattle Times,* December 3, 1999, p. A25.

Anon., "[WTO] Conference Ends, Protests Don't," *Seattle Times,* December 4, 1999, p. A7. Street protestors demanding the release of jailed protestors surrounded the King County jail. Other protestors chained themselves to the doors of the Westin Hotel.

Dunphy, Stephen, "WTO Group Will Leave Seattle With No Accord," *Seattle Times,* December 4, 1999, pp. A1, A5.

Miletich, Steve & Bartley, Nancy, "3 Charged With Felonies From Protest on Tuesday," *Seattle Times,* December 4, 1999, p. A7.

Anon., "Clueless In Seattle," *The Economist,* December 4, 1999, p. 17. "It is hard to say which was worse—watching the militant dunces parade their ignorance through the streets of Seattle, or listening to their lame-brained governments respond to the 'arguments'."

Anon., "The New Trade War," *The Economist,* December 4, 1999, pp. 25-26.

Anon., "Countdown to Ruckus [in Seattle]," *The Economist,* December 4, 1999, p. 26. A look at the "...Ruckus Society and assorted other fringe groups..." demonstrating against the WTO meeting in Seattle.

Anon., "Who Needs the WTO?" *The Economist,* December 4, 1999, p. 74. "For anybody who supports liberal trade, the mere possibility that the WTO might now become a cause of economic retardation is deeply disturbing."

Egan, Timothy, "New World Disorder: Free Trade Takes on Free Speech," *New York Times,* December 5, 1999, Section 4, pp. 1,5.

Kahn, Joseph & Sanger, David E. "Seattle Talks on Trade End With Stinging Blow to U.S." *New York Times,* December 5, 1999, NE, pp. 1, 14,

Sanger, David E. "The [WTO] Shipwreck in Seattle," *New York Times,* December 5, 1999, NE, p. 14. Why was the WTO meeting held? "...because Mr. Clinton was convinced that he had one last free-trade victory left."

Acohido, Byron, "Deal Struck to Free All Jailed Protesters on Own Recognizance," *Seattle Times,* December 5, 1999, pp. A1, A16.

Solomon, Chris, "[Anarchist] Squatters Vacate Downtown Building After 'Deal'," *Seattle Times,* December 5, 1999, p. A17. The deal involved the partial expropriation of private property in favor of units of the building to be put aside for the "homeless."

Anon., Letters to the Editors of the *Times, Seattle Times,* December 5, 1999, pp. B7-B8. Two pages of letters mostly from local residents but with a sprinkling of letters from across the nation. Interspersed on the two pages were two political cartoons and two photos. One of the photos had a caption showing an individual who had thrown a garbage can into a Starbucks' store window and then was photographed entering the store through the window. The initial portion of the caption was entitled "A WTO protester..." Even the editors of the *Times* had adopted the lexicon of the anarchists that the destruction of private property had become a form of "protest."

Wysocki Jr., Bernard, "The WTO: the Villain in a Drama It Wrote," *Wall Street Journal,* December 6, 1999, p. A1.

Cooper, Helene et. al, "WTO's Failure Bid to Launch Trade Talks Emboldens Protesters," *Wall Street Journal,* December 6, 1999, pp. A1, A17.

Waldman, Peter, "An Anarchist Looks to Provide Logic to Coterie at Core of WTO Vandalism," *Wall Street Journal,* December 6, 1999, p. A17. An interview with John Zerzan, the guru of the anarchists who destroyed property in Seattle. Mr. Zerzan was coy as to whether he was involved.

Irwin, Douglas A. "How Clinton Botched the Seattle [WTO] Summit," *Wall Street Journal,* December 6, 1999, p. A34.

Goldsmith, Jack L. & Yoo, John C., "Seattle and Sovereignty," *Wall Street Journal,* December 6, 1999, p. A35. The authors note with irony that the same groups opposed to the WTO for its lack of democratic controls favored the Kyoto convention imposing restrictions on countries as well as human rights treaties that would bypass Constitutional safeguards for American citizens.

Editorial, "Liberals and Social Order," *Wall Street Journal,* December 9, 1999, p. A26. "It was Mr. Clinton, several weeks before the [WTO] event, who said in the course of a very long news conference that he was glad the protesters were going to Seattle and that their grievances were legitimate."

Mitra, Barun S. "WTO Protesters vs. the Poor," *Wall Street Journal,* December 9, 1999, p. A26. "Then there was the young lady who looted a downtown shop while talking on her cellular phone...a desire to impose their own Luddite vision on the rest of the human race. Choice is anathema to these activists."

Krauthammer, Charles, "President's Seattle [WTO] Stunt Completely in Character," *Seattle Times,* December 13, 1999, p. B4. Clinton derailed the WTO talks and gave aid and comfort to the street protesters.

Zimmerman, Rachel, "Seattle and Its Mayor Face Fallout from Disturbances at WTO," *Wall Street Journal,* December 13, 1999, pp. A2, A10.

Pelley, Scott, "The New Anarchists," CBS-TV, *60 Minutes II,* December 14, 1999. Interviews with the anarchists who smashed store windows in Seattle during the WTO meeting. Pelley did not ask who elected them saviors of the planet or their refusal to accept responsibility for property destruction by wearing masks.

Anon., "The Real Losers," *The Economist,* December 11, 1999, p. 15. "These five billion live in the developing countries, and include the poorest of the world's poor. They are the real losers from this whole sorry episode [of protest in Seattle]."

Anon., "A Global Disaster [at WTO meeting]," *The Economist,* December 11, 1999, pp.19-20.

Anon., "The Non-Governmental Order: Will NGOs Democratise, or Merely Disrupt, Global Government?" *The Economist,* December 11, 1999, pp. 20-21. Self-appointed special interests groups from Greenpeace to organized labor pose threats to legitimate governments.

Anon., "NGOs" Sins of the Secular Missionaries," *The Economist,* January 29, 2000, pp. 25-27. More often than not, governments finance NGOs!

Carter, Mike & Postman, David, "Unrest Even at the Top During [WTO] Riots," *Seattle Times,* December 16, 1999, pp. A1, A24. There were sharp disagreements by federal, state and local officials on how to deal with protesters.

Eure, Rob, "Seattle is Again Besieged, This Time by ACLU, Other Post-WTO Suits," *Wall Street Journal,* January 26, 2000, pp. NW1, NW3. Eure writes "For Seattle, the World Trade Organization hang-over is just beginning."

Phillips, Michael M. "A la Seattle, Activists Target Davos Economic Summit," *Wall Street Journal,* January 26, 2000, p, A17. Phillips writes "The social and environmental activists who helped sink last year's Seattle trade talks are now converging on the ultimate elite party: the World Economic Forum...in Davos, Switzerland."

Zebrowski, John, "WTO Protest Leaders Plan Disruptions in D.C., Los Angeles," *Seattle Times,* March 4, 2000, pp. A1, A12.

Stecklow, Steve, "How a U.S. Gadfly And a Green Activist Started a Food Fight," *Wall Street Journal,* November 30, 1999, pp. A1, A10. A profile of Jeremy Rifkin and Benedikt Haerlin. "Genetically modified food, Mr. Rifkin predicts, will become 'the single greatest failure in the history of capitalism in introducing a new technology into the marketplace'." [This will occur only with the compliance of the media and the bandwagon of hysteria displayed over silicon breast implants, the Alar scare, nuclear power and tobacco!]

Huber, Peter, "Ecological Eugenics," *Wall Street Journal,* December 20, 1999, p. A26. The writer reviews a court suit against Monsanto on anti-trust grounds. In his view, they don't hope to win (but led by Jeremy Rifkin) they seek a platform and publicity. Jeremy Rifkin "wants nobody in the genetic technology business at all." The ratio of land for food to land for people occupancy is 6 to 1, higher in poor countries. PH also reports that North America now absorbs more carbon dioxide than it emits! And has more forested land than in 1920! [As Luddites they seek to stop gene research as well as its application. Or in essence "ecological eugenics" we abort this now!]

Powell, Jim, "Why Trade Retaliation Closes Markets and Impoverishes People," *Cato Institute*, Policy Analysis, No. 143, November 30, 1999, pp. 1-83. In a wide-ranging article the author reveals that foreign aid and lending as opposed to free trade has often unintended and negative effects upon the recipient nations.

About the Author

Currently, the author is a writer and an occasional arbitrator of consumer disputes for the Better Business Bureau.

Formerly, he has taught history and economics on the high school level; additionally for six years he taught adult education classes. On occasion he taught in-service professional classes to teachers. Also, he has served as an occasional instructor in the School of Education at the University of Washington.

For a decade as hearing examiner, he conducted student disciplinary hearings for the Seattle Public Schools. For three years he also chaired hearings of parental appeals of mandatory student busing assignments.

As to formal education, the author received his bachelor's degree from Queens College; and both his master's degree in economics as well as his doctorate in the history of education from the University of Washington.

Finally Garland published in 1996 his historical study, The *Schools in the Great* Depression. In 2000, iUniverse.com published his primer, *Games of Persuasion: Exercises in Media Literacy*.

* * *

www.ingramcontent.com/pod-product-compliance
Lightning Source LLC
Chambersburg PA
CBHW020237290526
45784CB00003B/1005